The
Queendom
Within

The Queendom Within

Rewrite Your Fairy Tale and Create Your Own Happily Ever After

Heidi Hauer

For all the women who seek true love,
while courageously building
fulfilling lives for themselves.

First published in 2021 by Heidi Hauer
in partnership with whitefox publishing

Copyright © Heidi Hauer, 2021
Illustrations by Marie-Thérèse Czapka

www.heidihauer.com

ISBN 9781913532321

Also available as an ebook: 9781913532338

Cover design by Emma Ewbank
Back cover photography by Wendy Yalom
Interior page design and layout by Anna Green / Siulen Design
Edited by Dawn Bates
Project management by whitefox
Printed and bound in the UK by Bell & Bain

Contents

Introduction

The fact that you've picked up this book tells me you've already devoted quite a bit of energy and time seeking love and happiness in a romantic relationship. You've searched high and low for your prince. Having done the same, believe me when I say I know *exactly* where you are coming from. And there is nothing wrong with looking for love in a romantic relationship – it is the most common place where we expect to find it, but it can be found in many other places too, and not least within yourself.

In this book I am going to show you how to create the life of your dreams starting from within, from a realm inside yourself – your very personal Queendom. This book will boost your confidence, build up your courage, and encourage you to follow your heart and listen to your intuition as you pursue and find your own happiness. Then, if Mr Right comes along, he'll join you in a life you already love.

To find out if this book is right for you, see if you can relate to any of the following scenarios:

✦ Maybe your life isn't quite matching up to what you had in mind. By now, you had hoped – planned, in fact! – to be happily married with kids. For whatever reason, it hasn't worked out that way.

✦ Maybe you have that sinking feeling that you're in the wrong life, as if you are in someone else's movie. Do you ever feel like you're in the wrong relationship, the wrong friendships or the wrong job? Are you silently hoping that Mr Right, once he arrives, will launch you into the life you are meant to be living?

✦ Maybe you're not entirely sure of who you are, but you know you need to change. Are you feeling the pull to try something new, shake things up and enter a new chapter in your life, while you're still single? Are you done with waiting for the long-promised 'happily ever after'?

✦ Or perhaps you're fresh out of a relationship. You know you've changed, but your life matches the old you, not the woman you are today or the one you could become. If you are ready to move on from past relationship patterns but unsure which direction to take, this book is for you.

Whatever is calling you, by picking up this book, you're already on the path to finding it.

What you seek, is seeking you.

RUMI

Through a set of 28 core plus 2 bonus exercises, you're going to set strong foundations for your Queendom brick by brick, step by step. By the end of it, you'll be looking at a very new reality.

This book will bring you to your truest self. The stories and activities are designed to help you get clear about who you are and what you want from life. Practical tools will encourage you to get creative and have fun. The programme I've created calls you to invest your time and energy in yourself. Along the way, your prince may come – or not. But there's a good chance that you'll be able to relax and release your need to control the outcome of your story so your own fairy tale can come alive.

My dream is for you to realise that you have choices in life and that everything you're seeking is already within you. That may sound a little cheesy, but it's absolutely true! It's time to venture into the unknown and embrace the life you're craving. I know you're ready.

A vision for a new way of living

Wouldn't it be wonderful to live in a world where all women naturally feel empowered to be who they want to be – where women are free to express themselves and their gifts, and shape the world in a way that is good for all of us?

A world where women don't depend on a romantic partner, nor on the hope of soon finding the right one to save them. A world where women don't define themselves purely through their profession or social status, or through their role as a mother, daughter or wife. A world in which self-confidence isn't impacted by the number of likes and followers on social media.

These days, you probably live in circumstances where the conventional deal between men and women is no longer the only option. Jane gave Tarzan her beauty, body and babies and in return she received food, shelter and protection. But we're no longer in the jungle nor in the Dark Ages. As women make their own money, they depend less on their partners to meet their physiological and safety needs. With options about when and how to raise children, women's needs in a relationship and what they look for in a partner have changed. If physiological needs are met, psychological and self-fulfilment needs gain in importance.

> **Women, you are not rehabilitation centres for badly raised men. It's not your job to fix him, change him, parent or raise him. You want a partner not a project.**
> JULIA ROBERTS

However, while practising physical and emotional independence by living and being on your own can be liberating and empowering, it does not have to be the only answer nor the ultimate goal. Independence and freedom are clearly preferable to dependence, but there is a fine line between being in your full power and rocking your life like a modern-day heroine versus shielding yourself away from the outside, hiding in an ivory tower in an attempt to avoid being hurt, or feeling you have to prove to the world that you can make it on your own. If you expand your desire for independence too far, you might unintentionally be too reserved; too emotionally unavailable for others. A strong strive for independence is the other side of the coin of dependence and is always an 'away from', whereas inner freedom enables you to move 'towards' something you desire. Wholeheartedly saying YES to whatever truly feels good to you will enable you to deal with the consequences of your commitment.

My dream is for you to be fully anchored inside yourself where peace, strength and love are *always* available. I wish for you to experience yourself as a creator of your life, not as a bystander watching from the sidelines or a background dancer in someone else's performance. You have every right and reason to be comfortable and confident as you graciously navigate your path through the world. Don't project your desire for connection onto a prince in the distant future. Connect and be yourself *in the here and now*.

Gratitude is a wonderful practice for appreciating what you have and who you already are. The simple fact that you are reading this book is an incredible privilege. Dedicating time to self-development was an inaccessible luxury for generations of women who came before us, and still is for many women on this planet today. If this work ever gets overwhelming or scary, just remember you're doing it for them too!

Hitting romantic rock bottom

My story starts with thirteen long-stemmed roses: twelve red and one yellow. He handed them to me with a soft smile and said, 'Each single red rose is a heartfelt thank you for every year we've spent together. I loved every moment with you but now we have to say goodbye to each other. The yellow rose tells you that I will always be there for you, whenever you need me.'

Ouch, that hurt. It felt like a punch into the stomach. But I knew he was right. The emotional rollercoaster we had been on for the past years was too painful, too energy-consuming and too toxic to sustain. The rational side of me was fully aware that this relationship had no future, but that didn't relieve the pain I felt in that moment.

Our highs had felt so amazing that I couldn't imagine myself with anyone else but him. To my friends who had watched the various facets of our dramas unfold over the years, concerned about my emotional wellbeing, I explained our relationship as 'the luxury of passion I allow myself in my twenties.' Now that I was in my early thirties, I had tried to end the relationship a few times, but with little success. The make-up sex was too good, and our emotional dependencies were too intertwined for me to walk away with a feeling of closure.

He explained that he needed to end our relationship so that he could find himself. As he spoke, I noticed how broken he seemed inside, and it hurt me to see him so lost. We parted ways that day. With the help of excellent therapists and coaches I began the process of healing my broken heart. I processed the relationship and realised that, despite some dysfunction, we had felt a strong love for each other and that it was OKAY for things to change because life is like a river – a constant stream of new events and experiences and after one chapter comes another. One day, I knew, I would find love again.

After a substantial amount of personal development work, I decided I was finally ready to meet and marry Mr Right and have kids. After pondering for a while about the best approach on how to address this 'project', I concluded that the most efficient way to achieve my new goal was to sign up to an exclusive dating agency. I assumed it wouldn't take long until Mission Husband Hunting was accomplished. I was confident that I would soon find myself walking into a bridal salon with a friend, sipping champagne as I picked my dress for the big day. 'Come on,' I thought to myself, 'It can't be that hard for me to find a guy.'

A full year and many dates later, I finally accepted defeat. Maybe divine timing cannot be outsourced to an account manager at a dating agency. Slightly frustrated, I decided to put on hold the job of looking for Mr Right.

Concocting a Plan B

Although I continued moving forward with the rest of my life – work, friends, personal development – I didn't feel truly alive. In fact, I felt more like Sleeping Beauty; I was existing, but in a petrified, frozen state. Life was happening around me, but I wasn't truly engaged. In all honesty, I was waiting for my prince to appear and kiss me awake. I had arranged my life as if it were a temporary solution so that as soon as he turned up, we could instantly ride into the sunset together and start our family – a dream I wasn't yet prepared to ditch.

Most of the time, I remained confident. During my trial-and-error attempts with men, I met frogs, knights, pirates, players, healers, noblemen and kings of foreign lands. But I had met love multiple times, and that had left me with incredibly high standards. I considered it a good thing that I wasn't willing to settle for anything less than a loving, caring, emotionally mature and mutually supportive partnership.

In my worst moments, on the other hand, I fell into self-doubt and anxiety. What if the arrival of the man I am destined to be with is poorly timed with my biological clock? What if he never finds me?

Perhaps his internal navigation system simply won't catch up with my many home moves across Europe? Or is he already on his way, just tangled up in the brambles that protect my castle?

At some point I realised that, prince aside, my real life was massively off-track from my dream life. The Kingdom had fallen apart while I was just lying there, waiting. I needed a Plan B for my life. I had to take matters into my own hands. It was time to become my own prince, wake myself up and create the solo edition of the Kingdom I had dreamed of building together with him. In short, I had to build my own Queendom.

Was I even ready, anyway?

As I looked towards creating my Queendom, a new question suddenly surfaced. Was I truly ready to meet Mr Right? I started imagining how I would introduce him to my life if we were to meet back there and then. My imagination took me to as a series of dates.

On our first date ...

'Hello, beautiful princess,' he might say. 'And so, we meet at last. Supposedly, we are a match made in heaven. So, who are you? Tell me about your life.'

And because my life mainly happened in the office, I would have started there. 'My life? Well, let me tell you about my job … The truth is, I have big dreams and I was waiting for you. What I would really love to do is … '

He might then ask me what I did for fun. 'Hobbies? No, I don't have any at the moment. I have to admit that I am addicted to work. It's somehow comfortable and easy not to think about anything else in life but work projects. But now that you're here, I can finally start pursuing my dreams such as writing. I'll start skiing again, too. I'm a bit out of practice. You surely love skiing and go all the time. So just let me know when you're ready to head up the slopes!'

On our second date . . .

'I am so sorry for being late! Blow-drying my hair is a forever hit-and-miss for me. But don't worry, now that you're in my life, I'll start being on time. Would you like to join me for an evening with friends? A bit of warning in advance: I have some very good and close friends and then also a random mix of people with whom I don't really connect well; I just picked them up at various stages of my life. But now that you're here, we can make new friends together! Let's choose inspiring, uplifting ones who do meaningful things with their lives and share our values. In fact, I expect you already have friends like that, and I can't wait to meet them.'

On our third date . . .

'It's lovely to see you again. I apologise in advance for being a bit grumpy; my head is heavy because I was out partying. I was lucky to hear the alarm clock go off this morning. I am starving! Work was so busy today that I only had time for salty afternoon snacks. Don't worry! Those aren't red flags, because now that I've met you, I'm planning to pursue a healthy and active lifestyle. Anyway, come in. Welcome to my place. It's a bit of an IKEA showroom; my mind was constantly in the office. There was no time to turn my apartment into a cosy and comfortable home. Also, I didn't want to invest in decor that you might not like. But in the meantime, I created Pinterest boards on furniture and homes I love. Let us look through them together.'

On our fourth date . . .

'Wow, this is so romantic. But can we turn the lights off, please? My underwear is pretty basic and I'm a bit ashamed of it. I saw no point in investing in expensive lace lingerie. But don't worry, now that you're here, I'm ready to order loads of hot stuff!'

Now, it's possible that my Mr Right would feel crushed by all that pressure. But even if he managed it well, he would have trouble getting to know me, because I was stuck somewhere between the person I had once been and the person I wanted to be. So many of my dreams were either still in their infant stage or not even born yet. The problem was that I was no longer in my teenage years. Already in my mid-thirties, my biological clock was ticking loud and clear, especially as having a family was still something I longed for.

I realised that Plan B – Queendom – wasn't just a quick fix to help me deal with Mr Right's delayed arrival. I needed to evolve into the woman I deep down in my heart knew I could be – not necessarily for his sake, but for my own.

The truth behind my fantasy

It was time to look at my fairy-tale fantasy a little more deeply. In the old days, all a princess had to do was wait patiently in her castle while her prince navigated seven mountains, defeated a fearsome dragon and cut his way through thorny rose bush brambles to reach her. That classical princess role description doesn't translate into modern times. As a strong, independent woman, I was ready for an updated version of the traditional fairy tale. Version 2020+ probably meant that as the modern-day princess, I had to muster up the courage to clear my own brambles, face my own dragons and climb all seven of those mountains.

That image led to a major question. Although I held such a clear vision of myself, I had done absolutely nothing, nada, niente to move my reality into that desired direction. Why had I pressed 'pause' in so many areas of my life, and why was only Mr Right allowed to press the 'resume' button? Only with a brutal level of honesty, deep down in my subconscious, well-hidden inside, I discovered a truth that was hard to accept at first:

I didn't just want a prince to save me. I wanted him to fix me – and my life.

In that fantasy, the moment Mr Right leaned forward to lay a kiss on my lips, my life magically transformed . . . without me having to do any of the work myself. No gardening, dragon fighting or mountain climbing required.

The second I realised that this is what I had been waiting for, I saw my mistake. This was a fairy tale on steroids. No Disney dream team could have come up with such a megamix of fantasies like the one that was subconsciously ruling my life. How could I ever find a guy to meet my standards when my own life fell so far short of them? How could I so willingly give my power away to someone I hadn't even met yet? Why did I not believe in myself enough to address the issues on my own?

A wave of shame washed over me. How was I so off track from reality? I felt like hugging this poor guy and apologising for all the expectations I had thrown at him before he could even wave hello. And I realised that the pressure I had put on 'Mr Right yet to be met' – the expectation that he would turn both me and my life into something I liked – was, in fact, the brambles surrounding my castle. Hiding who I really was from the world will make it impossible for him to find me. The only way to attract him into my life was to fully step into my dream life and show up big time for what I desired so that he could see, hold and love me for who I really was.

Now, I am not sharing all this to embarrass myself publicly. I am sharing it because if you are reading this book, it's likely some part – large or small, known or unknown – of you might recognise yourself in my story. If so, don't feel sad, hopeless or ashamed. Rewriting your fantasy is possible, and I'm here to walk you through it.

Though uncovering this fantasy is a bit uncomfortable, let's not waste time blaming Disney, society, our parents or basically anyone else for its creation. It is what it is. Disney's fairy tales simply put pressure on a wound that we all share. The only useful question is: where did that wound originate?

We all have a deep-rooted subconscious sense of oneness, unity and unconditional love. We know this feeling; we remember it from before we were even born. The prince of our fantasies represents a short-cut to that feeling; the fast-track; a bridge to something far bigger, way beyond ourselves; something magical, eternal. But life isn't about quick fixes or taking the easy way out. Here's the catch: we are having this human experience so that we experience ourselves as we climb up the ladder to awareness, self-realisation and, ultimately, enlightenment. We would spoil the fun if we let anyone else remove the hurdles and challenges that lead to essential life lessons, specifically designed for us. Instead, it's up to us to figure out our purpose in life on our own, to tap into and develop courage as we go about realising what we came here to experience.

How to use this book

Two sets of exercises

Through a set of 30 steps, this book will show you that the magic lies as much in the journey as in the destination. The results you get will depend on how deep you allow yourself to go as you work through the exercises, each of which is designed to be completed in one day. You will benefit most if you stick to the suggested sequence and don't skip exercises. Transformation processes are highly individual and it's totally normal that some exercises will resonate with you more than others.

With that in mind, each exercise comes with an optional 'Diamond' level exercise to help you dive deeper. They are called diamond exercises because going deep into a transformational process will bring you the clarity, confidence, strength and sparkle of a diamond.

As the diamond exercises are more profound, completing them will probably take you longer than a single day. That's okay. Your personal transformation is not a race. This is your life and you can decide how much depth and attention you apply to each step. You might want to spend a few days extra on an exercise that is particularly exciting for you, or you might want to slowly pace yourself, giving each part an equal share of your undivided attention. Some readers will finish the entire programme in a month; others will take longer.

Find a pace that's both motivating and nourishing. Let the lessons sink in, but don't let yourself get stuck. Whatever pace you choose, it's important to take one step after the other. The learnings in this book are designed to build sequentially. In some exercises I will ask you to capture your dreams and write down insights, observations and reflections. You might treat yourself to a beautiful new journal that makes you smile every time you pick it up.

If you do choose to fast-track this programme, pick a time in your life that is relatively calm so that you can pay full attention to your growth. The exercises are very powerful and will certainly have an impact on your life, immediately and in the long term.

Three foundational blocks

In order to support you to move through this programme and get everything that you want from it, here are three foundational blocks that will help you build your Queendom . . .

1. Choose to participate

My biggest dream is for you to realise you have choices. Participating actively in this programme is one of these important choices. This book is in your hands for a reason – remember why you chose to say YES to this experience. If it was a gift to you, embrace it with open curiosity.

Seize each opportunity to create a life you love, irrespective of whether you have a partner or not. Choice is always available to us. Even if we try to keep everything the same, we're actively choosing to do so. The options available to us might not always be exactly what we want or feel that we deserve, and yet they are still there. Sometimes the only choice we are left with is how to react to a given situation. The act of choosing how to experience, frame and remember a specific event is courageous and powerful. This is a step towards choosing your experience of life, which brings me to the next foundational block . . .

2. Venture into the unknown

Even though it might not always be obvious, there is usually a solution to every challenge. When it comes to creating the life, work and relationships you truly desire, you will often be required to step outside of your comfort zone. This is usually the territory of the 'unknown'. Navigating the big unknown and re-emerging exactly where you want to be, takes courage and consistency.

Pushing yourself outside your comfort zone can be hard and also fun. The exercises within this programme are designed to be accessible. Be fine with facing uncomfortable emotions from time to time. Feeling a bit challenged is an excellent sign that you are doing the work. This is what self-development is all about. When you are coming up against a wall of resistance don't stop but instead, challenge yourself to step into that unknown. Welcome the uncomfortable growing pains as exciting signs that you're doing something different. This is what you're really here for, right? This is where the final foundational block comes into play . . .

3. Trust the process

Through any journey of change, there will be times when you want to rest, take a different path or give up entirely and return to what's familiar. That's normal. Getting back on track and moving forward is all that matters. Trust in yourself, your vision and your capabilities. Trust that the world will provide you with exactly what you need, even if these gifts appear as challenges, roadblocks or hard lessons to be learned.

When we trust the process, we know that the destination is approaching as soon as the time is right. This is true even when we can only see one step ahead of us on the path – or no steps at all. Life is full of opportunities, but timing is everything. Do yourself a favour and add patience to the mix.

> **Those who are certain of the outcome can afford to wait, and wait without anxiety.**
> A COURSE IN MIRACLES

Follow your instincts and the inspirations that randomly come to you. Get curious about the people who unexpectedly turn up in your life. Step into the cafes, public parks, online communities and bookshops that call for your attention. Read the books that fall off the shelf or that are recommended to you by several sources. Say YES to the serendipitous experiences that appear out of nowhere. This is trusting the process; it's listening to the language of the Universe, which guides you towards the things that will keep you on your path. It doesn't matter whether you believe in God, energy, intuition, destiny, soul-purpose or spirit guides; trusting the process transcends anything religious, because it's just a shift in the way you choose to perceive your relationship with the world around you. It doesn't matter where exactly your messages are coming from; if they're coming to you, trust them.

Four parts

This programme is broken into four parts of seven exercises each, with two bonus exercises at the end. Here's a breakdown of what you can expect in each one of them:

Part I: Meet the Real You

In Part I you will rediscover and define in detail who you are and what you want out of life. I invite you to go on an inner journey of self-reflection. This kind of practice is essential in our modern world, where we're often encouraged to be externally focused and 'in our heads' about everything. To uncover our deepest dreams and goals, we have to engage our heart. In this first part we enter the world of intuition, inspiration and desire. During this process of reinventing yourself, you'll begin to identify and review your current beliefs about life. This will open the door to a much deeper and more empathic understanding of why you think and feel the way you do. You might find it's time to leave behind some of the beliefs that are blocking you.

Part II: Dare to Shine

Part II is all about practising how to be authentically you and feel fantastic about it when you're on your own. You'll take the new things you learned about yourself in Part I and channel them into inspired action. But don't worry, we'll take it step by step! This part is all about how you're showing up in your immediate environments. Think self-care, nutritious and delicious food, and comfortable surroundings. But don't be fooled, it's harder than it sounds. Shedding old behaviours and upgrading how you care for yourself can bring up a lot of resistance. So, take a deep breath because it's time to transform and thrive!

Part III: Prepare for the Show

Being yourself when you're alone is nice, but if that's the only time you're authentic, it's neither sustainable nor will it substantially change your life. To build an inner world and an outer world that you actually want to live in, your actions have to match your aspirations. In this part, you'll start to understand how your current relationships and environments are influencing you. You'll see who and what is taking up your energy or lowering your confidence, and where your behaviour isn't exactly mirroring your true self or wants. This is all about standing firmly in your power. Are you ready? Of course you are!

Part IV: Play it for Real

While Part III was mainly about awareness, Part IV will guide you to step up and step out as your true self into the world. This is where you'll learn about boundaries and protection. There are two reasons why this part is a make-or-break for the entire programme. First, you need to shine your own light again. If you are around people who dim your light, whether they're conscious of it or not, you've probably started to only share the smallest version of yourself with the world in order to stay safe. In this case, shining your light, even though others might not always approve of it, is the learning opportunity here. Second, you need to learn to sustain that light. Building up a life that is fulfilling and nurturing takes time and focus, especially at the beginning of your conscious creation journey. Being clear about your boundaries as you engage and interact constructively with others is not a task for one weekend, it's a life-long practice. So, in Part IV, you'll be doing what can often feel scary: being seen and heard as you set clear boundaries. Be brave, be loving and be kind to yourself as you venture out into a new life. These steps won't be easy, but neither is hiding in the shadows. I would even say, it's easier to take little courageous steps over the next few weeks than to let yourself be boxed or pushed by others into a life that doesn't feel like yours.

Bonus Exercises

After Part IV, there are two bonus exercises designed to help you bring your learning forward and ground everything you experienced in the other exercises.

Creating your Queendom

Building your Queendom is about discovering and expressing yourself authentically, standing up for yourself, building, dismantling and recreating your life. It's in our own emotional, mental and spiritual evolution that we find joy and happiness. Our dreams are carrots on a stick that are meant to move us forward towards expansion. Evolution through expansion is the real name of the game.

Creating your life by yourself is ultimately far more exciting than being rescued by a prince. During this process you experience yourself as the creator and shaper of your life, which is a liberating act of empowerment. If you don't know who you are, you're about to find out. If you have put certain dreams on hold, you'll first reflect upon the reasons behind that and reassess if they are still your dreams. Only then are you open to receive what is meant to be yours.

As you go through the exercises in this book, I recommend you to take a break from dating. Whether you do the programme in thirty days or longer, let it be all about you for a while. There's a strategy behind this. Before you meet your Mr Right, you want a solid, authentic, real foundation in your life. If there is a wide gap between who you are today and who you imagine yourself to be, you are dating with two faces, and that's a recipe for disappointment. That's why it's time to bridge the gap by first learning to accept, celebrate and love yourself in the present moment, just as you are. Then, when and if your Mr Right comes along, you can dream and realise even bigger and better visions for yourselves together.

Shortly after realising that I was waiting to not only be saved, but also to be fixed, I reached out to a friend who was facing similar dating woes. One of the sparks leading to the creation of this programme was a longer dialogue on that subject I had with her. For one month we challenged each other daily with fun tasks that helped us to become more self-confident around men who we were attracted to. In the subsequent eighteen months, I dove deep into all the aspects of my fairy-tale expectations. As I developed and implemented the exercises in this book, I tamed inner demons, faced my fears, solved inner conflicts, overcame obstacles, resisted temptations, and ultimately made peace with myself and the world around me.

And it worked! The small actions and decisions I took at that time shifted things around in a good way. Life went from predictable and restrictive to inspiring and expansive. I felt more confident and fulfilled than ever, even though the newly set 'big goals' were still a long way off. This was a version of me that felt real and alive. It was a me that was adventurous, optimistic, calm, grounded and excited about life.

Little did I know that this experience marked the start of another path, one that would see me become a dedicated Holistic Health & Life Coach. With that, dear Princess, consider yourself 'kissed awake'. Now, let me guide you towards creating your Queendom.

✦

✦

Part One

Meet
the
Real
You

Once upon a time, there was a princess, determined to reinvent herself . . . By the time I proactively started my personal transformation process, my problems transcended the romantic. On the outside, everything appeared to be perfect. I had a great international career, my social calendar was thriving, I exercised regularly and treated myself to retail therapy when I was feeling down. It was the *Sex and the City* reality that most of my peers aspired to attain.

On the inside, however, frustration was bubbling. I had moved to Zurich a few months earlier. All of the people I had met suddenly didn't feel like *my* people. The honeymoon that comes with moving to and exploring a new city was over, and my social groups felt shallow to me. There was fun and glamour on the surface, but little emotional connection beneath. I experienced the same flat feeling in every aspect of my life, as if there were an invisible barrier stuck between me and the world. I felt like I was simply watching my life move past me without really being part of it. The love and connection I had expected felt further away than ever.

One day, I found myself venting about this to a friend. How could it be that I had 'everything', but I still didn't have what I really wanted? His response was blunt: 'You don't even know what you want!'

It hurt, and at first, I tried to ignore his input, but over time the comment lingered. It felt like he had poked at a wound I hadn't known was there.

'So, what *do* I want?' I asked myself. 'And who *am* I to want it?' With regards to my career, I was good at setting and achieving goals. Unfortunately, this skill didn't translate well into my personal life. I desperately tried to figure out the goals for my personal life in my head, not in my heart. And my soul didn't buy the story. My life formed an impressive image, but I longed for more depth and genuine connection. It showcased what I did and had achieved, but not who I was as a person. The *real* me wasn't visible in the life I had created. The trouble was that I didn't really know the *real* me. Ouch.

Consider it the other way around. If you dated a guy in his forties who was constantly dreaming about everything that he imagined becoming one day, would you fall in love with him in his current or future version? You would probably think to yourself: 'Grow up, man. It's already halftime in your life. What are you waiting for?' I used to love men for their potential, until I learned that you have to take them at face value and love them as they are. You get what you see. If you get more later on, lucky you, but don't count on it.

My sense of fairness told me that I cannot ask of others what I am not prepared to deliver myself. I realised that it was up to me to turn things around and move my life in the desired direction. Luckily, I had some tools to lean on. I had already found the world of personal development. As I read and learned about manifestation, energy and the power of the mind, I came to realise that my own inner thought processes were rigid and restrictive. For instance, I had developed a robust and critical filter system that tore apart or undermined every desire, idea or potential passion that took me out my comfort zone. I decided to start a new experiment: I allowed myself to dream up the most amazing, exciting, inspiring life I could possibly imagine through unapologetically listening to my heart's desires.

I spent six months giving the creation of that dream as much space as I could. The only rule I set myself was to daydream without judgement or self-criticism. I thought about what I really wanted instead of what I thought I needed. I fantasised about my perfect day, my dream partner, and how I would contribute my skills to the world. What would my lifestyle look and feel like? I saw myself playing with my kids in the living room of my ideal home. Instead of storming right into action with the aim of making the low-hanging fruit of that dream come true, I paused, probably for the first time in my life, and let the vision expand even further in my mind. I gave my dreams the space and time they needed to tell me what I truly wanted.

Once I had that figured out, I started writing down small but significant actions I could take to move towards the life that had revealed itself to me. It was crystal clear that if I continued on my current path, my dream life would stay a dream. I knew I needed to create massive shifts for things to change. Being comfortable outside my comfort zone needed to become my new norm.

Today, I focus on maintaining and enjoying a state of inner peace. I practise being kind to myself and others. I know who I am now, and it's my daily choice to act from a place of alignment with my true self. On some days, it's easy; on others, less so. But I show up every day with the intention to honour and enjoy my journey.

The magic can only unfold when you consciously choose to connect with who you really are. Loving the authentic version of yourself is the first step to creating your Queendom.

Don't be a Queen waiting on a King.
Be a Queen busy with her Kingdom
until her King arrives.
ANONYMOUS

STEP 1:

Uncover what is calling you

Draw a road map of your desires

Before you start building your inner Queendom, you first need to know who you are, what you stand for and what makes you YOU.

This is actually one of the hardest things to find out because you have to mentally single yourself out from the crowd in order to identify what is unique about you – look at yourself through the magnifying glass called honesty. Even the idea of standing out from the crowd can be scary and make you feel vulnerable, open to judgement or like you don't belong. This is totally normal. For human beings, the desire to fit in is literally written into our DNA. It's a natural survival instinct that tries to keep us safe.

Granted, our wish to 'fit and blend in' is really useful in potentially harmful situations, but when nerves are stopping you from doing something you truly desire, it's time to put fear aside and explore a new experience. Let's get real. How do you expect to love your life if you're constantly resisting or actively hiding who you really are?

> **She remembered who she was,**
> **and the game changed.**
> LALAH DELIA

EXERCISE 1

Grab your journal and a pen. Write down all the things that you really want to experience in your life, irrespective of what other people might expect of you.

Create two columns. One for the small dreams in life, which could be anything from baking bread to sky diving, from buying yourself flowers to speaking up in meetings, from taking up ballet classes to running a triathlon, from attending a retreat to composing a song. Here, put ten things that bring you joy, make you smile and uplift your spirits.

The second column is for your big dreams, such as moving to another country, writing a book, starting a family or setting up a charity. Here, put three things that you would love to experience in your life.

As you work on this list, listen to your heart, not your head. Try to avoid writing down dreams that your parents, partners or others may have for you. It's not about them, it's about YOU. Add to the list whatever comes up, irrespective of how crazy it might seem.

You know what's coming next . . . it's time to check off that list! Pick one thing from the small dreams list that you can make happen today or within the next week. While intention always comes first, practical planning leads to action. Consider what it will take to implement your task and write down what you need to organise to get it done with ease and joy. Then go for it.

Next, reflect upon which mindset shifts you may need to make to enable your big dreams to come true. Break your big dreams down into small steps and start implementing them.

Challenge yourself to come back to this list every Sunday as you plan for the upcoming week. Keep adding ideas as new desires arise. Take on new small dreams and continue working towards your big dreams. Your dreams are like little seeds. Don't expect everything to blossom overnight. It takes nurturing and patience to grow them into the plants they are meant to be.

DIAMOND

Address the blockages between you and your big dreams. Work with a coach or therapist you trust on identifying and removing or reframing beliefs that are standing in your way. For example: What is the fear behind starting a family? Why do you think that following your passion is not a real life choice you can make for yourself?

Dive into fantasy land

Imagine being someone else

Most of us have found ourselves daydreaming about an imaginary life. 'What would I do if I won the lottery?' is a common, fun and revealing question to contemplate and explore. This is now an opportunity to 'try on' different lives in your mind to see what fits best.

Thinking about realities that may never come to pass could be seen as a sad or a counterintuitive thing to do. You will discover that there is value in it and that it's actually really fun. It's time to let yourself imagine …

> ### The measure of a great life is whether it matches your dream.
> MARIE FORLEO

EXERCISE 2

If you could miraculously live three different lives, what lives would you choose? Grab a pen and paper and answer the following questions:

+ What work does this alternative person do in the world?
+ What does their typical day look like?
+ With whom do they share their life?
+ Where do they live?

- ✦ What do they do with their leisure time?
- ✦ What are they passionate about?
- ✦ What values, issues or campaigns do they stand up for?

Once you're done, look over your answers for those three different lives and further reflect on the following:

1. Why did you choose these lives?
2. What specific elements draw you in the most?
3. How can you integrate a little of those elements into your life today?

DIAMOND ✦

Bring elements of those hypothetical lives into your own to get a taste of what it would feel like. For example, if you were dreaming of being a painter, join a class. If you'd love to be an actor, find a local theatre group and join the fun. Find ways to bring a flavour of those other lives into your own.

Mix the soundtrack for an amazing life

Uplift yourself through music

Music has a powerful influence over our energy and emotions. Just a couple of beats of an amazing tune can drive a spark of motivation straight to our gut; a single, beautiful melody can easily bring us close to tears. We know this. We've experienced this. So why not use it to our advantage? Why not sound-design our life? Let's not accept the default settings of a busy life as given. You don't have to wake up to the sound of a terrifying alarm that puts you under stress before you even get out of bed. On your way to work, do you really want to hear loud traffic and listen to terrifying news? Instead, use the playlist you create here as both an alarm and the soundtrack to your commute, filling your world with the type of sounds you most want to hear.

Dear Music,
Thanks for always clearing my head,
healing my heart, and lifting my spirits.

LORI DESCHENE

EXERCISE 3

Create a playlist packed full of powerful songs that make you feel amazing. These will be the tunes that never fail to wake you up, get you moving, motivated, inspired or support you to tap into a positive, go-getting energy. Start with a base of ten songs on a programme like Spotify or iTunes and add more tracks over time.

Keep it somewhere accessible and play it on your way to work, before an important event, when you are at the gym or getting ready to go out with friends. If scintillating vibes are the background music of your everyday life, you might just find you'll consistently feel as if anything is within your reach.

DIAMOND

In addition to a playlist that hypes you up, create other playlists for different purposes: one that calms you down, another that enhances your concentration and focus as you work, and one with meditative sounds and mantras that helps you to centre yourself quickly and puts you in touch with the magical world beyond the mundanity of everyday life.

Go time-travelling

Take a peek at your future life

Life is made up of so many 'should haves'. By the time we hit school age, we are already full of conscious and subconscious messaging that illustrate what a rewarding, successful or valuable life should look and feel like.

Without even realising it, so many of us strive towards the 'should haves' without ever explicitly asking ourselves, 'Do I really want this?' The answer may be yes, but this isn't always the case. The more you make your choices consciously, the less you'll end up on autopilot heading to an undesired place, only to later be bewildered that it didn't bring the happiness you expected.

> **Don't feel stupid if you don't like what everyone else pretends to love.**
> EMMA WATSON

EXERCISE 4

Are you ready to travel into the future? Get comfortable on your sofa, snuggle up in a blanket, sip a calming tea, close your eyes and play some music that helps you to relax.

Imagine you are looking into the eyes of your eighty-year-old self. This 'future you' smiles and sends you love. She has lived her/your dream life and is excited to offer you the wisdom that will help you to

find your path. Sit with this vision for a minimum of twenty minutes. As you sit, try to feel the happiness that she is so easily radiating. Invite her to share the story of her life with you.

Ask your future self how your life will unfold from now on . . .

- ✦ Where in the world has she lived? Where is she now?
- ✦ Who has she spent her life surrounded by?
- ✦ What adventures has she had?
- ✦ Does she have children? If so, how many?
- ✦ What is her wisdom on romantic relationships?
- ✦ What lessons has she learned or what hardships has she overcome?
- ✦ What has she done for work? What career has she had?
- ✦ Which three words would summarise her life?
- ✦ What advice would she give you regarding the struggles you are currently facing?

Take as much time as you need to connect with your future self. When you are ready, come back to the present moment and try to carry that wonderful and soothing feeling that you might have experienced into your day.

DIAMOND

If you enjoy writing, grab a pen and journal. Put on relaxing music and write for at least twenty minutes. Let your words and vision flow onto paper without judgement. Go deep. Don't leave anything inside. Later, if you're feeling a little lost in life or are struggling to fully understand what you really want, come back to these notes as a form of inspiration.

If you're more of a visual person, create a vision board. Cut out images from magazines that you are drawn to and stick them into a collage or use Pinterest to create boards online that visualise your dream life. This process might take a bit longer, but don't force it to be picture perfect. What matters is the mood that those images ignite in you, not whether the house or garden or husband on your board look exactly like the version in your vision. Keep your online boards secret if you don't want to share them with the world.

Feel free to evolve and amend the vision board as you get to know yourself better during this programme, but don't constantly change everything. The images place seeds in your subconscious. They require nourishment, attention and patience so that they can grow and ultimately blossom into beautiful flowers. Look at your vision board daily, ideally first thing in the morning, and feel the joy and happiness that arises from seeing the pictures you have chosen.

Get inspired

Seek out role models

While living life on your terms requires courage to be independent and a desire to be free, no human being is an island. Drawing in guidance and camaraderie from others is a beautiful way to build a community and gain valuable lessons and inspiration from those you admire. One way of doing this is to seek out your role models – strong, relatable and inspiring people who motivate you to witness and nurture the greatness in yourself. Also, give yourself permission to be a role model for others.

> **Be the kind of woman that makes other women want to up their game.**
> ANONYMOUS

EXERCISE 5

Aim to find three people who are living the lives, embracing the values or creating the experiences that you feel deeply drawn to. If feelings of envy come up because you would love to have what they have, know that everything you admire in someone else is already within you. In your mind, cherish and celebrate that person. Connect with them and observe how they live that specific quality that you would like to develop in yourself. Think and act from a place of abundance, not scarcity. These could be people in your own life. They could be family members, colleagues, friends or even individuals you've observed from afar. They could also be people you've never met or who are no longer alive; for example, your ancestors, historical or public figures whose stories deeply resonate with you. Get creative, and if nobody comes to mind, get researching!

Once you have selected three people, write down exactly what you love about them and consider how you can embody their energy or behaviours in the way you make choices and show up in your own life, work and relationships. Make a board with pictures of your role models and look at it whenever you need inspiration and a reminder that anything is possible.

DIAMOND

Connect yourself deeply with your role models. Try reading a biography or watching a biopic if they are public figures; consuming their content if they are creators, such as reading the books they wrote or going to see the masterpieces they painted; or by being in their presence more often if they are people that you know. The goal is to understand their key to success and to get a feeling for how they think about life.

Let the outdoors in

Take a walk outside in nature

Sometimes relaxation and re-energising looks like wearing stretchy pants, curled up on the couch, watching a couple of TV dramas, and that's okay. However, if we're constantly (and unconsciously) numbing out in front of the TV, even this seemingly nourishing habit can become the very thing that de-energises and drains us. It's a blurred line between relaxing to re-energise and hanging around because we've become too lazy to move around.

There are many times when what we really need is to simply clear our minds. Through pressing pause on the input and the messaging that is constantly coming your way, you can create space for your thoughts and emotions to get the attention they deserve. These are often the moments when the most significant hits of clarity and inspiration pop into your mind.

Deep in the forest I stroll
to hear the wisdom of my soul.

ANGIE WEILAND-CROSBY

EXERCISE 6

Take thirty minutes in the next few days to take a walk outside with no agenda, no purpose and no errands to run. Just enjoy the journey and allow yourself to 'be'.

If you have access to natural lands or a park, head there. Nature really is a powerful space of healing. If the city is all you can access right now, find a calming space to walk. Head into a quieter neighbourhood or a place where you love to get lost. Observe your surroundings and the people around you with a child-like curiosity. When you've finished your outing, set a timer for three minutes and write down any thoughts and feelings that arise.

DIAMOND

Arrange for a weekend in nature. Perhaps a hiking trip or time at the beach. Use a free weekend within the next two months to find stillness within yourself through connecting with nature.

Reassess traditions

Make up your own mind

Traditions, customs and beliefs influence many different aspects of our lives. They can come from family, communities, institutions, societies and any place that has had an impact on how we think, feel and behave.

Beliefs around traditions are often anchored in our subconscious, handed down from the generations that came before us. That doesn't mean that everything in your life has to be set in stone. You have the power (and right) to set your own traditions. You can choose which rules, beliefs and behaviours you wish to celebrate and which ones to ditch once and for all.

Being flexible in regard to creating new ways of living and celebrating is wise when it comes to starting a new life with a romantic partner, but also a useful skill to apply when you are single. If your original family is a rock-solid nurturing space that you can always rely upon, then you might now want to take even more time to connect with them. If you either don't have such a background to connect to, or you don't want to be in touch so closely, turn your friends into your family.

As traditional family and societal structures are breaking up, conventional forms of connection are becoming looser and looser.

We can either lament the change and despair about the downfall of the world as we know it or celebrate this freedom and realise that it's our duty and responsibility to create nurturing circles around us. In the same way as we change our beliefs around family and friends, we can also adjust our beliefs about life in general.

> **There are friends, there is family,**
> **and there are friends that become family.**
> ANONYMOUS

EXERCISE 7

Today you are going to unearth some of the subconscious messages that may be influencing the way you currently think, live and act. Grab your journal and a pen. Write down the most relevant stories, beliefs or experiences you've witnessed or picked up related to any of the following areas:

+ Cultural or annual festivities and celebrations
+ Family
+ Friends
+ Romantic relationships
+ Travel
+ Money
+ Work and career

Here are some examples of beliefs that might trigger your process of reflection:

+ New Year's Eve always has to be the biggest and best party of the year.
+ Family is there when I desperately need support, but otherwise I go about my life without them.
+ Friends come and go. They are nice to have but don't require special attention.

- ✦ Healthy eating is expensive and home cooking takes a lot of time.
- ✦ Work has to be the number one priority, no matter what.

Use short sentences and don't overanalyse what you write down. Trust whatever comes up first; these are often your strongest subconscious beliefs. Set a twenty-minute timer for this exercise if you tend to lose yourself in childhood memories. Aim for three beliefs per area. When you finish, read back over everything you've written and ask yourself the following:

1. In which ways have these messages so far influenced my life or the way I think about and generally behave in these areas?

2. Look closely at the beliefs and customs that you feel have had a negative impact and then ask yourself: How can I change the narrative? What would I love to do that could form a new tradition?

✦ DIAMOND

Take specific action to test out new traditions and play around with familiar beliefs. If you would like to make changes to certain festivities, such as hosting a Christmas dinner with friends, plan ahead to do so. What about the weekends? Do you feel most lonely on Sundays because you believe that this day is reserved for families only? Think about starting your own tradition, such as Sunday brunch with other single friends or having movie nights on Sundays. Take action to test how it feels if you do exactly the opposite to what your family traditions or conventional beliefs would suggest you do.

✦

✦

Part Two

Dare

to

Shine

I found myself looking around my flat thinking about how much better my home could look once Mr Right and my real me had found a new place together. After all, my vision boards showed pictures of my loving husband and wonderful children in a beautiful home.

What else was on my vision boards? Well, for a start I'd have a flawless body, of course. I'd be fit, toned and energised for our passionate sexual encounters. This would all be happening on my dream box-spring bed, next to a nightstand with beautiful white, fresh flowers. Our furniture would be an exquisite blend of family heir-looms, modern pieces and pictures we had collected through our shared love of art. He'd definitely be into health and wellness, and we'd regularly go on health and meditation retreats together. We'd host dinner parties for our friends and we'd have a life full of joy, laughter and magic.

In other words, my life would look and feel completely different. My surroundings would be more sophisticated, my habits and behav-iour would be bolder and more authentic, and my life would reflect the lightness and inner freedom I had gained during all those years of personal development work.

Yes please, I was ready for the big vision of my life to become reality. So, what did I do as I was waiting for Mr Right to find me? I resisted buying furniture that I wanted and needed. I put off booking holidays, to make sure I had enough time for a partner in case he would soon come into my life. I nurtured a space of transience to avoid arriving anywhere 'final' without my man in tow.

It was out of pure frustration and boredom that the truth finally hit me: I didn't have to wait! And nor did I want to wait any longer. I wanted to feel amazing, not tomorrow but today. How was it possible that my life was so out of alignment with the life that I actually wanted to live? It was time to bring the authentic me back into my life. I turned my frustration into decisiveness and stepped into the version of me that I had hoped to find through Mr Right.

With many tiny as well as big and bold actions in nearly all areas, I started turning things around and took the driver's seat of my life. I started going to retreats on my own. I bought myself flowers. I said YES to exciting opportunities that came my way and I embraced them wholeheartedly. Most importantly, I stopped leaving vacant space in my life for a partner I hadn't met yet. Instead, I started filling that space with activities and things I loved. No more postponing my dream life forever and a day. This cautious approach to life had to stop.

Feeling good about yourself and your life as it is in the present moment is what living in alignment is all about, and what we'll explore in Part II. Alignment is about responding to what the real you wants and needs. We don't wait for the perfect external situation; we create a situation that feels authentic from the inside. When it comes to smaller things like buying yourself flowers because you like them, having a bath when you want to, eating your own banquet, wearing sexy underwear because it makes you feel attractive or visiting new places on your own, you might be thinking, 'What's the point? Surely I should only focus on my work while I wait for Mr Right, so I can move ahead in my career as fast as possible before we meet. Why create a life now when it will eventually come to me anyway? Surely most things are better when you have someone else to share them with?'

Maybe, and sometimes. But here's the thing: alignment keeps you on the path to a life of deep fulfilment. If we make daily choices to feel our very best, we can expand our life and reach our goals in a loving, sustainable way. Meaning? Through building up your life around your dreams and desires, you draw good things closer to you. Living fully in the moment is actually the only way to get what you want. Your dream life will never just fall from heaven, wherein all you have to do is unwrap the gift. That's an illusion. We all have to build our lives for ourselves brick by brick, whether we are women or men, single or in a partnership.

> ## You get in life what you have the courage to ask for.
> OPRAH WINFREY

As you construct your Queendom, piece by piece, you learn to call what you want into your life and get rid of what's not working. Ready to get started? Let's delve into Part II . . .

Your home is your castle

Get creative in the home

Having a long-term vision for your life is an inspiring way to keep you working towards what you really want. However, often we get so caught up in looking ahead that we forget to address the smaller but equally life-altering choices that enrich our everyday experiences.

When you really think about it, life is basically one big journey. Sure, the stopovers and milestones can make it pretty exciting, but in reality, enjoying the ride is the most important thing of all. And that journey happens now, in this very moment. Don't postpone feeling amazing until the day you sit in your picture-perfect life. That day might never come, especially if you don't learn to feel good in the here and now.

**A house is made of walls and beams.
A home is made of love & dreams.**

ANONYMOUS

EXERCISE 8

Home should be a place where we really feel . . . at home! It's our own little pocket of the world where we can nourish ourselves, relax, rejuvenate and nurture our sense of belonging.

You don't need to live in your dream 'forever home' in order to connect with this vision. There are always ways you can create an environment that allows you to flourish and grow. Make your home reflect who you want to be. Turn your home into a 3D version of your vision board. Put the past behind you and focus on your future.

Here are some ideas you could implement:

- ✦ Decluttering your life starts with decluttering your living and work spaces. Get rid of anything that is no longer serving you. Who needs all the study books from your college years? Are those gadgets from the nineties really worth keeping? If you are sentimental about a particular piece, either use it intentionally or wrap it up nicely and put it in the attic.
- ✦ Organise yourself so that you find things when you need them. A tidy space allows your mind to be at ease and creative.
- ✦ The trick is to declutter your home regularly. According to Feng Shui, decluttering around the full moon is especially powerful because it's the time to release any old energy. Set a reminder in your diary for the next six full moons to declutter new areas in your home or go to a deeper level of decluttering. It's absolutely refreshing and it's much easier to walk into your future when your luggage is light.

DIAMOND

Now that you have less clutter, look at other ways of refurbishing and fixing your home:

- ✦ Repair any broken things around your home that have been bothering you. If you are, like me, not a DIY expert, don't feel guilty asking for help, or book a handyman. The feeling you get from living in a home where everything works will be worth it.
- ✦ Freshen up your surroundings with a lick of paint, new furniture or beautiful visuals, such as printing off and framing your favourite quotes, ordering some prints or art, or simply choosing new screensavers for your devices.

- ✦ Add in more comfort with cushions or throws, better lighting, a more supportive desk chair, a laptop stand, a bedside table, etc.
- ✦ Bring the outdoors in. Invest in some plants or visit the most gorgeous flower shop in your city. If you want to go big, order a weekly bouquet of flowers to be delivered to your door.
- ✦ Introduce your favourite scents through candles, incense or diffusers with essential oils.

Dine like royalty

Enjoy your own banquet

Eating great food isn't just about nourishing your body, it is also about nourishing your spirit. When we embrace it, cooking offers abundant opportunities for joy, love, happiness and peace. It can be a time to switch off, stimulate your creativity and introduce a special slice of luxury to your day.

If you're on your own, or not that inspired by the kitchen, it can be tempting not to bother. We often fall into the trap of just eating whatever is quick and easy, as long as it fills us up. Sometimes this is fine and pretty unavoidable. However, choosing to consciously slow down and look at, smell, taste and enjoy food is an amazing way to fill your life with mindfulness, self-care and beauty.

> **I know what I bring to the table.**
> **So, trust me when I say I'm**
> **not afraid to eat alone.**
> ANONYMOUS

EXERCISE 9

Ready to dine like royalty? Here are ways you can weave more love and consciousness into this area of your life:

+ Prepare a dedicated area. If you can, set up a dining table that's especially for eating. It doesn't have to be grand; just a place where you can always sit down for meals without having to clear a space.

+ Make it look pretty. Treat yourself to a nice tablecloth, charger plates and linen napkins if you use them. Treat yourself to a shopping tour to speciality stores where you can get personal advice. Put a vase of flowers or a plant in the middle of the table or create your own centrepiece.

+ Awaken your senses. Look at your food in anticipation and appreciation before you take the first bite. Smell everything before you put it into your mouth, savouring its unique scent. Close your eyes as you chew and enjoy your meal.

DIAMOND

+ Eat what you love. Inspire yourself to cook by preparing your favourite foods. Open a cookbook and pick a recipe for a meal that makes you want to eat right away. Cook it either today or at the upcoming weekend. Once in a while visit a special delicatessen food market, buy yourself something luxurious, such as a special kind of dark chocolate, exquisite truffle brie, high-quality tea, exotic fruit or something that is not part of your standard grocery shopping list.

+ Get the right equipment. Invest in cooking and kitchen equipment that makes preparing food enjoyable and stress-free. It doesn't have to be expensive, just practical and supportive for what you love to cook.

✦ Add a luxurious touch to your dining experience. Invest in timeless dinnerware and cutlery. A beautiful setting upgrades the entire experience. It incentivises you to cook with higher ambitions and to sit and chew more mindfully and for longer.

✦ Hold dinner parties. Enjoying delicious food in the company of wonderful guests at your nicely decorated home can lead to memorable evenings. The time and work you put into it will be worth it! Think of meals that can be prepared in advance so that you can enjoy the evening too.

Give your body what it wants

Offer tender loving care

In our modern, fast-paced lifestyles, physical self-care often stays on our to-do list and never gets the attention it deserves. Listening and responding to what our body needs, and building a close relationship with it, is usually something we have to learn. You may even feel a lot of resistance to it and avoid it by telling yourself that you don't have time for such an activity. Be compassionate with yourself because being disconnected from or unhappy with your body can bring up feelings of sadness, shame or discomfort.

Whatever your current relationship with your body, one thing is for sure: it will stay with you for your whole life. The sooner you nurture a loving relationship with it, the happier your life will be. This point is invaluable for your love life. The amount of love, appreciation and respect you bring towards your body shows how you want to be treated and will define how someone treats you – and this is particularly true of intimate partners. The chances of your body being adored, caressed and passionately seduced by a lover are much higher if you love your body unconditionally every day. How you treat yourself sets the tone for how others treat you.

EXERCISE 10

What does your body currently long for in terms of physical self-care? The answer can vary from day to day and depend on what makes you feel amazing, sexy and alive.

Maybe it's applying some moisturiser or drinking more water. Maybe it's going to bed earlier, cancelling appointments if you are too stressed and overworked, getting a haircut or a massage, doing some stretching, soaking in the bath, or acknowledging your sexual needs and desires.

Pay attention to where you are in your menstrual cycle. If you are having your period, allow yourself to rest and take things slowly. Notice your biological rhythm. When during the day do you have your natural energy peaks and when do you usually experience the lows?

Whatever comes to mind, prioritise two acts of self-care today or work them into your schedule as soon as you can. The more you respond to your body's needs, the more the practice of self-care will become a natural part of your day.

DIAMOND ✦

Set up a specific schedule for you that prioritises physical self-care. What times of the day are best for you to have breakfast, lunch and dinner? How often does your body need exercise? How many hours of sleep keep you sane and grounded? Do you need a monthly acupuncture session to balance your energies? Make sure you arrange your schedule in such a way that your needs are met before they become apparent. Listen deeply and organise activities accordingly. Try this out for one month and then keep what is working for you.

My temple is my body. My world around me, my altar. My words are spells. Every thought an intention. My actions, rituals to manifest all that will be. I am SACRED I am DIVINE.

ARA

Dress to impress
. . . yourself

Filter out the masks

Have you ever felt that spring in your step when you're rocking your favourite outfit? Or have you ever felt that awkwardness when your clothes don't sit or fit right, or you're wearing something that looked good on the mannequin or model, but really doesn't reflect the true you?

What we wear can be a powerful expression of who we really are. Our attire can positively elevate our mood and comfort levels and increase our self-confidence. Our style is one way of outwardly communicating our personality and energy, which helps us attract people and experiences that align with who we are. It's important, though, to play the game of fashion in a way that serves you, that makes you shine, that amplifies how amazing you are. Remember, you are the centrepiece, not your latest bag.

Let me stress that this is not that 1950s' kind of advice, which says, 'Don't let yourself go when you are single. You must always brush your hair before leaving the house!' It's no news that nice appearances are more attractive, but all I wish is for you to feel amazing simply for your own sake.

I cannot think of a better representation of beauty than someone who is unafraid to be herself.

EMMA STONE

EXERCISE 11

Arrange a block of time within the next week to do a wardrobe clear-out. Select each item one at a time and run it through this checklist:

- ✦ Did I wear it within the last twelve months?
- ✦ Does it fit well right now? (This is a tricky one. Watch out for that voice that tells you if you lose/gain weight or suddenly wake up with a different body shape, that dress will look good!)
- ✦ Is it comfortable? Do I like how the fabric feels?
- ✦ Does it make me feel good about myself?
- ✦ Do I like this style?

If you answer 'no' to any of the above, it's time to donate, sell or gift it. If you haven't done this in a while, going through everything you own can take some time. If this exercise seems far too arduous, start with just one category such as tops, trousers or shoes. Put on music to make it more fun or invite a friend over whose fashion advice you find useful to help you with choosing what should stay and what should go. Once I did this a few times, I made a habit of going through my entire wardrobe twice a year, in spring and autumn. I found that approach far more manageable!

DIAMOND

You might find that you need to invest in a few more personalised items. Before you do, get really clear about what you love and what you don't. Online research or Pinterest are both great places to start.

Check out the personal shopping services of high-end department stores close to you. This experience is often for free or tied to a minimum shopping expense and might help you to find what suits you best. If you're able, book an appointment with a personal stylist. This can be an incredible and eye-opening experience as you learn to understand what really suits your body type and your character!

Be bold,
be beautiful!

Make a playful statement

Sometimes the smallest thing can make us feel unstoppable: red lipstick, fantastic boots, a statement piece of jewellery, a new hairdo or playful underwear.

While it can be seen as fickle, physical items and fashion statements can spark an inspiring energy within us, helping us to feel bold and fully in our power. When we're already feeling great, the right accessory or excellent make-up can electrify our mood. When we're feeling kind of flat, it can inject a little life and oomph to help us own the day.

> **Beauty to me is about being**
> **comfortable in your own skin.**
> **That, or a kick-ass red lipstick.**
> GWYNETH PALTROW

EXERCISE 12

It's time to make a statement. Style yourself in a way that makes you step into your superpower. If you don't own a red lipstick, go out and buy one just for the fun of it. You don't have to have an important meeting or special date to put on clothes that make you feel fantastic.

The idea here is to treat one day as a special fashion and style day simply because you decide to make it special.

Don't panic – there's no need to get overwhelmed with this exercise. It doesn't need to be a grand affair and I'm not asking you to rock a ballgown if you are usually in activewear. It's more about the conscious and mindful attention you pay towards what you wear, how you do your hair, what kind of make-up you put on or which shoes you choose. Especially if you usually prefer it more laid-back, easy and low-key, this exercise will challenge you to step outside your comfort zone.

The most important element of this exercise is not to treat it as another attempt to get attention or approval from others. It's about celebrating being a woman and honouring your natural beauty. It is all about cherishing YOU. Set the alarm clock twenty minutes earlier so that you enjoy this exercise before you start your day. Be bold, be brave and have some fun with it!

Conversely, if you are someone who is usually very well put together and obsessed with your appearance, this exercise is about doing the very opposite. Today, as you meet friends or go to the office, I encourage you to feature a look that is as natural as possible. If leaving the house without a perfect blow-dry or a full glam make-up is hard for you, dance to an empowering song before you present a more natural version of yourself to the world. Believe me, you'll survive this experiment.

DIAMOND

Extend this exercise to an entire week. See how the way you think and feel about yourself changes and observe how people around you react. After that week, decide which elements you want to integrate into your normal routine.

Be your own cheerleader

Talk to yourself with love

Finding a supportive network of friends is an important endeavour, and one that you'll explore in Parts III and IV. However, no matter how mindful you are about whom you spend time with, there will only ever be one fixed voice that consistently sits beside you: your own. If this voice is forever putting you down or saying, 'You're not good enough,' you'll always be swimming against the tide when moving towards the things, relationships and experiences that you really want.

In the dark, you find yourself.
INANNA, THE QUEEN OF HEAVEN AND EARTH

EXERCISE 13

Learning how to capture negative thoughts and transform them into positive ones is a practice of self-awareness. It takes time, but it gets easier as you reap the benefits. Do this exercise as often as you can, aiming for a minimum of three times a day. Set alarms for three days in a row to remind you in the morning, at lunchtime and after dinner. When the alarm goes off, take a moment to listen to the voices of your thoughts. Then, address them with this simple three-step approach:

1. Witness the way you speak to yourself (try not to judge what you hear).
2. Reflect upon why you may have had that thought.
3. Rephrase it. Choose something more positive and supportive to say instead.

Here's an example:

1. **Witness your thoughts:** e.g. 'My colleague's work is so much better than mine. I am not good at my job and should just give up.'
2. **Reflect on why you are feeling the way you do:** e.g. 'Hmmm, I guess I'm feeling like I'm far behind my colleague, and disappointed that I'm not further ahead by now.'
3. **Rephrase your thoughts in your mind:** e.g. 'My work contribution is unique and valuable. I will reach my career goals at the right time for me.'

It will feel weird and fake at first, but it is absolutely worth the effort! Your aim should be to become so aware of your self-talk that you constantly observe it in parallel to everything you do. Become your own cheerleader and you will be unstoppable.

DIAMOND

Keep a little notepad in your handbag or use the notes app on your phone to write down the negative thoughts that cross your mind throughout your day. The most difficult part will be to catch yourself while you are thinking in patterns that you've probably been carrying around for years or decades. Make a habit of this and continue observing your thoughts as long as it reveals new information to you. Then, become super clear on your most destructive thought patterns. Once you've identified them, start reframing them every time they come to the surface.

Ultimately, you want to be in a continuous self-coaching mode in which you witness without judgment, analyse and redirect your thoughts in a self-loving, self-nurturing, self-supportive way. Speaking to yourself with love and care has the power to positively transform all of your experiences.

Explore a new horizon

Venture out on your own

Visiting new places is a great way to feel inspired, enjoy an adventure and create diverse, long-lasting memories. Today, the virtual world has evolved into such a common place to hang out that many of us have become very disconnected from the physical world around us. To truly connect with our surroundings, it helps to explore new cities, sights and places. While doing this with other people is undoubtedly fun, when we believe this is the only way, we can limit our experiences. Getting out on a solo adventure is an incredible and empowering step to claiming your happiness.

> **A strong woman looks a challenge dead in the eye and gives it a wink.**
> GINA CAREY

EXERCISE 14

In this exercise, you'll explore somewhere new. Choose a day trip to a local town, city or neighbourhood you don't know well. Or you may want to visit a new exhibition at your favourite museum, or a park, sight or attraction you haven't visited yet. Explore two new places over the next three weekends. Capture in your journal what you saw, heard and felt, as well as how this experience affected you.

DIAMOND

If you're feeling brave and have the means, why not organise an entire weekend away on your own to a place you haven't been before? Challenge yourself to do something fun that's just beyond your comfort zone. Make sure that the place you pick is safe and that you are protected. Never do something that you are completely uncomfortable with. This exercise is more about finding places you would like to go, but that you might not otherwise visit without a friend. Pick a place. Then plan the trip, book it and go!

✦

✦

Part Three

Prepare

for

the

Show

I said goodbye to my friend, hung up the phone and slumped into my chair. This cycle had to stop. I knew that. But how? Surely friendship was about offering support. Was my desire to draw back just me being selfish?

A few days before, I was feeling excited about starting to write my very first book – this book, in fact! I was in the heavy waves of an increasingly demanding corporate job, so finding the time to fully switch off and commit to my passion project was something of a challenge. However, I'd cleared my deadlines and my diary. Sunday afternoon was all about creating space for my new life to emerge. I could feel the magic brewing. Knowing that I was finally putting desire and words into action was a big deal for me, even if I hadn't yet seen the fruits of my new labour. The intention was there, and I was ready to go.

Just as I sat down to write, I got a text from a friend. She was arguing with her partner and needed to chat. She sounded pretty upset and wanted to meet up. Well, I thought, I guess I'm technically free. So, I grabbed my bag and headed out to meet her for tea, pushing the writing to later in the evening. A one-hour meet-up extended to three hours, and by the time I got home I was emotionally exhausted. I felt like I had spent the entire time just feeling her pain, holding space for her and giving her the motivational talk she seemed to need at that point in her life. Yet it made sense to put my writing on hold; it felt great to offer support, and I was confident my friend was ready to make big shifts in her life. Although it wasn't exactly what I had planned, my afternoon was surely very well spent.

A couple of days later I called to check how my friend was doing. To my surprise, she acted like nothing had happened. In fact, she didn't really seem to know what I was talking about. She thanked me for being a reliable sounding board to let off steam and assured me that now she was fine! She was great! Life was back to normal! She had neither initiated nor implemented any of what we had discussed to improve her situation.

I hung up feeling pretty frustrated and depleted – not just with her, but with myself. How was I surprised, again!? This pattern is familiar to me. Friends called and I ran, eager to support them. I felt I was the go-to lady for everyone's drama. The one who cleared her diary, the one who listened and the one who never asked for anything in return. I realised that although I enjoyed giving advice and guidance and being there for others, I needed to make sure my friendships were well-balanced spaces full of mutual support, positivity and fun, with an uplifting spirit.

It got me thinking how some of my friendships no longer seemed the right fit for both sides. What I wanted for my life was changing; I was changing. I was certain that I couldn't carry on exactly as I was. I had noticed over the years that my female friendships had begun to serve as a space either to plan how to get a guy or how to be with someone. In some friendships, complaining about our boyfriends' impossible behaviours was adding extra strength to the bonding effect. I was tired of guys getting all the attention, even when they were not around.

It was time to discover new ways of being with my friends. I wished for my female friendships to be a space where we talked about shared interests, laughed and reflected upon life. I craved positive, uplifting, caring human connection beyond the social interactions

I had at the workplace. I was curious to see what sisterhood had to offer apart from dating advice. And I knew in order to find out I had to make the first move. My new intention? Bringing more mindfulness, curiosity and presence to current friendships and widening my circle.

I began inviting my friends to dinners and brunches at my place and seeing them in a far more holistic light than in the past. To my surprise and relief, moving conversations away from men and men alone was not as difficult as I had anticipated. As I shifted the focus away from dating and relationship talk, the nature of our relationship shifted.

This experience changed my perspective on friendships and female networks. For me, supporting women who do great work and have positive intentions is a given. If we keep each other small, and pull each other down, it will be an even longer struggle for women to step into powerful leadership positions. The only way forward is to support each other, not only through professional networks, advice and mentoring, but also through nurturing a clear vision where women constructively work together with men towards a better future for us all.

**A girl becomes a woman,
when she learns to love herself
more than she loves a man.**
ANONYMOUS

Are you looking to create more space for deep, supportive friendships that see and love the real you? The exercises in Part III await you . . .

Check your foundations

Build your castle on solid truth

The ground on which to build a castle is made of rock, not of sand. When it comes to building your dream life, the same principle applies. You can't create a life you love without a strong foundation of truth about who you are.

If you spend your life pleasing other people, living up to societal standards and expectations, you'll constantly find yourself trying to uphold an artificial reality. Don't be surprised if at some point the building crumbles or collapses if it wasn't a HELL YES from the beginning. The truth always shows its face eventually.

Your personal truth is your authentic self. It's who you really are. The first 14 steps of this programme may have brought to surface some deep-rooted, hidden dreams or even old wounds. It's totally normal to feel overwhelmed or confused about what you really need, especially after beginning the in-depth inquiry that building your Queendom requires. Let's help you find clarity.

You are the artist of your own life.
Don't hand the paintbrush to anyone else.
ANONYMOUS

EXERCISE 15

Know when to listen to your brain and when to follow your heart. The brain is a useful tool for coming up with strategies, testing the feasibility of ideas, reasoning, planning and executing efficiently. On the other hand, when it comes to setting the overall direction of your life and successfully nurturing relationships, the heart is the more reliable guide. Think of it as reading a compass and a map. Your heart is your compass, whereas your brain reads the map and figures out how to get you from A to B.

Over the years, your needs will change as your priorities shift. Your heart's desires evolve as you grow and walk through life. Some dreams last a lifetime, but they take different shapes and forms along the way. They are here to guide you through your life along a red thread. Then there are the more sudden ideas, desires and wishes. These can help you enjoy life to its fullest.

This meditative exercise is an effective way to find your personal truth:

+ Find a private space where you won't be disturbed for at least five minutes. You can sit (cross-legged on the floor or comfortably in a chair) or lie down on a couch. Keep your back straight and your weight evenly supported.
+ Place your hands in your lap or by your side. Make sure they feel natural and comfortable.
+ Start to relax your body by taking three deep breaths in through your nose and out through your mouth.
+ Ask yourself, either aloud or silently:
  'What do I really need for my happiness?'
  'What desires come from deep within my heart?'
+ Spend at least five minutes doing nothing else but focusing on your breath, asking the questions again if you feel called. If your brain starts running off in different directions, just come back to your breath. No judgement. No drama!

- Be open-minded about any answer that presents itself to you, including the possibility that nothing comes at all.

Find a minimum of six opportunities over the next two weeks to practise this exercise. With time, you will learn to differentiate between the voice of your intuition and the one of your ego. Intuition is kind, loving, gentle and soft. Fear directs your ego. It is reactive and can be intense. Over time, the truth will start to surface. How will you know? The truth is consistent, so the message you need to hear will come to you again and again.

DIAMOND

Meditate daily in stillness for ten minutes and in addition to the above two questions, ask yourself the following:

- What do I want for my life?
- What do I want for my relationships?
- What's the next step I have to take in my life to evolve further?
- What do I need to embrace to move closer to my heart's desires?
- What do I need to let go of so that I am lighter, freer and more open for new people, partners, projects and other joyfulness to come into my life?

Schedule dates with your dreams

Make space for your priorities

Fairy-tale lives aren't made of wishes, wants and faith alone. Sure, vision is key, but without action your dreams will stay just that: dreams. If you marry vision with action, you can change your life and the world.

The first step to action is finding time for it. There are only so many hours in the day. If your calendar is packed to the brim with stuff that is irrelevant in the grand scheme of things, change in the areas that matter most to you will never happen. It's time to make some space for the stuff that's actually important.

> ### She needed a hero.
> ### So that's what she became.
> ANONYMOUS

EXERCISE 16

Before you can position your life in the direction of your dreams, you need to know where you stand. Keep a journal or calendar, jotting down the activities that cover more or less every hour for a week. It's important to get clear about where you spend your time. If you already have a detailed diary, analyse a typical week of yours.

Score each activity on two dimensions – the degree of planning and the degree of desire for engaging in this particular activity – as outlined below. Give it a 1 or 2, then choose between A or B.

1. Pre-planned and intentional
2. Spontaneous and unexpected

A. I want more of this
B. I want less of this

Look over your calendar and consider how much of your time is spent intentionally, meaning you actively chose and planned it; and how much of it is dictated or influenced by external factors, meaning you were responding to other people's requests. A bit of both is natural. It's all about how it makes you feel and/or what else it's keeping you from doing.

Now make the changes and create space every week for time that is entirely your own. Even just one hour a week that is dedicated to your passion project can drastically shift your energy and propel you towards your goals. Use this time for anything you want, whether it is starting a new project, learning a skill or having much-needed rest. The only rule? That time is sacred. Schedule it and stick to it. Put your phone away, get rid of distractions and keep the date between you and your dreams!

DIAMOND

Schedule entire weekends or maybe even weeks for working on your passion projects. Create your life in a way that increases the 1s and As and avoids or prevents the 2s (especially the negative unexpected) and reduces the Bs. Make it a habit to go through your calendar for the week ahead every Sunday and add time blocks exclusively for achieving your dreams.

Hear what's not being said

Listen to your body

The words we use and the tone of our voice are not the only ways we communicate with the world. Our body talks in its own language without us having to say a single word. These more subtle messages have the power to attract people and situations into your life without you even knowing. They can also do the opposite and push people away.

Understanding and paying attention to your body language can give you priceless information about how you truly feel when you're engaging with someone else. Know that your body never lies. Its reaction to anything in life is always right in any given moment because your body lives in the present, not the past, not the future. Let's make sure this kind of magic is being put to use. Just remember that whatever you put up with, you end up with.

You meet the people you need when you stop needing the people you meet.

EMMA GRACE

Today you're going to start observing how your body feels as you navigate social situations. This will help you to get clear on the energetic exchanges that you might not otherwise notice. Watch what feels good and what feels like a message that you need to address. Bear in mind that body language has a unique touch and therefore needs to be interpreted within the context and case by case. The following grid gives some examples.

Comfortable body language	Uncomfortable body language
Natural, relaxed eye contact	Nervously avoiding eye contact
Respectfully taking up space, shoulders open, head raised, straight posture	Crossed arms, slumped shoulders, hunched back, head looking down
Confident, relaxed use of hand gestures	Erratic or excessive hand gestures
Leaning in and speaking in the direction of the person you are talking to	Constantly looking around the room, at your watch or at your phone
Affirmative movements e.g. nodding head and smiling in response	Frowning, bored expression
Relaxed, comfortable muscles and joints	Stiffness, rigidity or pain
Energised	Drained
Stable, grounded	Lightheaded, distracted

As you start to become more aware of your body language, capture your observations in your journal. Keep an eye on any patterns that emerge when being with the same people or within the same environments. What is your body trying to tell you? Deciphering your own body language takes time and might feel very strange at first. Be gentle with yourself and always stay curious.

DIAMOND

Once you've mastered awareness of your body language, try experimenting with consciously expressing how you want to come across – perhaps in a more confident, elegant or charming way. For example, sit up straighter than usual, make gestures in a slower or more graceful way, stand up or lean forward when you want to get your point across, to name just a few ideas. Play around with it and watch how others react and how it makes you feel.

Know that body language is powerful. Even the most subtle elements are picked up by your environment. It's important you are aware of how you can shape the image that people have of you. This exercise is not about being neat and nice and fitting in; it's about feeling empowered to create a version of yourself that feels good to you.

Some may argue for authenticity at all turns. I prefer being the master of when and how I share my authentic feelings. In a job interview or a tough meeting, you might not want people to see that you are nervous. If you find yourself in an uncomfortable conversation, using confident body language might help you use your voice and share your opinion more clearly and assertively.

Learn to listen

Keep your ears and heart open

A lot of people *think* they are good listeners, but many of us struggle to really stay present to hear what is actually being said and what not. Listening actively is deceptively hard in our distracted culture. It requires us to focus on the content and tone of voice of whoever is communicating with us, while observing their body language and resisting the urge to listen to our own opinions and thoughts. Often, our desire to evaluate the situation or give advice gets in the way of our ability to listen.

As you practise listening, learn how to use your mind and your heart. Or in other words, listen to understand, not to answer. Being heard and understood feels amazing and is a gift for everyone. Noticing how others really feel is key to establishing trustworthy bonds and supportive relationships. If you only hear the words, a conversation quickly becomes a transaction of sharing information, but it doesn't touch hearts. All human beings crave an exchange of deeply fulfilling heart energy. By intentionally and consciously creating connections with others, you will improve your relationships and nurture yourself at a deep level.

Use this skill of active listening not only to strengthen relationships that are already going well, but also to notice what is not serving you. If you hear something between the lines that does not come from a benevolent, loving and caring place or you feel that the energy

exchange is very one-sided, don't be shy to address it. This allows you to ensure that your closest relationships truly align with who you are and what you really need. And if it is clear to you that the person you are speaking to does not have your best interest at heart, take some space, physically and within yourself. Choose friends that nurture your heart and soul and offer them the same care and support in return.

True beauty in a woman is reflected in her soul.

AUDREY HEPBURN

EXERCISE 18

Start practising the art of active listening throughout today. Remember, it is a practice, so don't expect to excel at it straightaway. And bear in mind, this exercise will impact you as much as it will impact the person you're listening to. Here's how you do it . . .

- ✦ *Become physically engaged.* Position your head and body towards the person who is speaking and maintain comfortable eye contact throughout the conversation.
- ✦ *Stay focused.* When you feel yourself being distracted by your thoughts or what's going on around you, consciously bring your awareness back to the conversation.
- ✦ *Pause before you speak.* Slowly count to three before you respond (this may seem like forever, but trust me, it's not!)
- ✦ *Clarify what they've said.* Ask questions, paraphrase what you've heard, delve deeper and check whether you have understood the message they were trying to convey. Share your curiosity before you share opinions.

DIAMOND

At the end of the day, grab your journal and explore the following questions:

- ✦ How did it feel to practise active listening?
- ✦ What new things did you become aware of throughout the day?
- ✦ How did it affect your experience with others?

Write down the positive and negative experiences you had without being judgemental or without giving room to the desire and hope that you can change anyone. Instead, learn to draw your lines and reduce the time you spend with people who are not actively listening to you.

STEP 19:

Create your inner circle

Draw out the gatecrashers

As you discovered in the previous step, listening to others is an eye-opening experience. Now that you have your stronger listening skills, you can use them to get clear on what is being communicated to you through your friendships and relationships.

When people have been in your life for a long time, it's not uncommon to navigate your relationships on autopilot. When things are going great, this can be a beautiful comfort. But when damaging or less desirable behaviours are present, you can end up feeling stuck in dynamics that offer little support.

> **Each time a woman stands up for herself, she stands up for all women.**
> MAYA ANGELOU

EXERCISE 19

Make a list of five to eight people who you want to be surrounded by regularly. As an adult, your ambition should no longer be, for example, to hang out with the most popular kids at school. You want to have

104

people close to you who share your values and interests, who are supportive, who take you seriously and who believe in you.

If names don't come to you straightaway, use your listening and intuitive skills over the next week to get clear on who you want to have in your inner circle. Assess your interactions with the people around you to determine whether they leave you in a positive or negative mood.

This isn't about playing the blame game, as relationships are always an overlap of two people's choices. What you're doing is taking stock of your current relationships to see if they are truly aligned with what you desire and deserve.

Use your journal to reflect on what's important to you. You might find it useful to assess:

- ✦ Core values or beliefs
- ✦ Positivity vs. negativity
- ✦ Warmth vs. cold
- ✦ Shared interests or hobbies
- ✦ Emotional or physical availability
- ✦ Unsolicited feedback or criticism vs. valuable advice
- ✦ Controlling vs. supportive behaviour
- ✦ Expectations and assumptions
- ✦ Respect and appreciation

DIAMOND

Put pictures of the people you welcome into your inner circle onto one board or page. Look at this inner circle of friends and maybe family members for one minute every day for the next three weeks. As you look at them, put a hand on your heart and think of them with positive feelings. You'll be surprised about how much this little act will bring compassion and kindness into your life.

Practise graceful independence

Switch your tiara for a crown

Having the confidence to create a life you love isn't all sunshine and rainbows. Sometimes you will be faced with criticism, pushbacks, doubt and negativity from people around you. This can be especially true if your newfound confidence shifts dynamics in certain relationships or puts you on a path that requires significant change.

When someone doesn't support you in the way that you'd hoped, it's tempting to lash out, argue back or withdraw completely. True, this can feel good in the moment, and sometimes an argument cannot be avoided. However, the more energy you spend trying to change people's minds about your new choices, the less energy you put towards going for what you desire, building your Queendom with the people and experiences you truly want in your life!

It might be 'sexy' for a princess to throw a tantrum in her early twenties, and it will certainly attract attention, but it will not get you very far. We want to be Queens who use their hearts to set a clear direction and who use their minds to navigate through everyday challenges with calm, ease and peace.

It's absolutely impossible to control everything that's going on around you. Don't be tempted by trying to direct opinions of your friends, checking the actions of your colleagues, or controlling everything your kids might be doing. It's a fight you will surely lose. Instead, learn to master the sea of emotions inside of you. Finding and keeping an inner state of peace is worth more than any external validation.

Being gracefully independent means that you are happy with your own company because you are connected to grace. Your sense of self-worth doesn't depend on any form of external validation. While engaging with the outside world can be wonderful, your permanent residence is inside your heart. From that space, you navigate confidently and peacefully through life.

Do not look for a sanctuary in anyone except yourself.

BUDDHA

EXERCISE 20

Think about what you really want to draw into your life. Go back to Part I if you need to remind yourself. Chances are, some people in your life won't approve or 'get' it. It's likely that some of them will share their opinions in a way that might disappoint you; maybe they already have. Don't take it personally.

Grab a pen and your journal and write down seven potential criticisms from others that hold you back or make you doubt yourself. Then, go through the list and turn each one into an unstoppable statement! For example:

Potential criticism	Statements that keep me committed to my dreams
My colleague thinks I am not qualified for a position I want to apply for.	I have worked on a strong motivational letter outlining my relevant qualifications and I am confidently going to apply for a position abroad.
My Mum thinks I give up too early.	Her opinion is just one view amongst many. I acknowledge her doubts and follow through on my plan nonetheless as I am not prepared to stay in a toxic relationship any longer.
My friend thinks all vegans are undernourished.	I understand the advantages and concerns of choosing this particular diet. I will try it for two months and see for myself what will happen.

Negativity from others can considerably drag you down. It's even possible that your body holds onto negative emotions without you even knowing. Repeat this exercise anytime other people's opinions are bothering you. Getting them out on paper and flipping them around helps to neutralise them. Become so steadfast in your convictions that other people's opinions will not blow you off your path.

DIAMOND

Be crystal clear about why you are going after your dreams and how it will feel to have achieved them. Take a piece of paper and write down three reasons why your dreams are important to you. Add three motivational statements that you need to hear to give you the confidence to succeed. Write it onto your bathroom mirror with lipstick, put it into your purse or somewhere else you will see it daily. Read it out loud to yourself every day until hearing the statement feels totally normal and good to you.

Pursue a thrill

Stray outside your comfort zone

You've likely come across the sayings 'If you always do what you've always done, you'll always get what you've always got', or 'Nothing changes, if nothing changes', or 'Change begins at the edge of your comfort zone'.

Often doing something new can feel a little risky. Even if it's as small as baking bread, your brain might persuade you into thinking you don't have the skills or that your time could be spent on something 'more important'. We tend to associate courage with a single heroic act, when in fact, courage is required for even the tiniest daily acts outside our comfort zone. It's these acts that turn an average life into an amazing one. Ready to take a leap?

The only thing that is holding you back from living your life is fear. What do I mean by fear? I am not referring to the kind that makes you triple-check your parachute before you jump out of the plane. I mean the little fears that sneak into your everyday behaviours, such as those that stop you from asking for a pay rise or promotion, dressing in a way that makes you feel attractive, or fully sharing your sexual desires with your partner, and so on.

I am always perpetually out of my comfort zone.

TORY BURCH

EXERCISE 21

Grab your journal and a pen and set a timer for fifteen minutes. Write down everything that instinctively surfaces in response to this question:

If I weren't afraid, what would I do?

Keep writing for the full fifteen minutes. List the big and small things in all areas of your life. Now pick one thing you're ready to cross off right away! Look for something that's doable in the next few days and that makes you excited, or even a little nervous.

Now, don't back down. Put it onto your to-do list and into your calendar to ensure you make it happen. Challenge yourself to come back to this list every week until everything that you find the courage for is ticked off. If you want to go big, make it a habit to do one thing a day that scares you. Become highly aware of the areas where you hold yourself back out of habit.

Anything counts that takes courage in your world. What might be easy for one person is a big achievement for someone else. For you, courage might be smiling at a stranger that you feel attracted to, taking bootcamp classes in the early morning hours, going on a retreat alone, joining a painting class. Or it might be becoming active in your local community, cancelling your engagement to be married because it just doesn't feel quite right, or quitting your job to turn your passion into a profession. It's anything that you feel called to do.

DIAMOND

It takes true courage to look fear straight in the eye and do it anyway. Sometimes we need to understand where our fear is coming from, but sometimes the confidence we are looking for comes from taking action, even if we are not quite ready yet. Pick one big challenge that has been part of your inner dialogue for some time and just do it. Trust that you will learn to fly when it is needed.

✦

✦

Part four

Play
it
for
Real

It was the end of a busy day at the office and I found myself frustrated with a colleague. It felt like she constantly undermined me by keeping me out of the loop. As I reflected upon the situation, I suddenly realised I was limiting myself to only two scenarios: it was either all my fault, or all her fault. What I was doing was cunning. I was ignoring the third option, the hardest option: that we were both responsible for the unease in our relationship.

By perceiving it as just my fault, I could go away and deal with it without an awkward conversation. As much as she annoyed me, I didn't want to upset her. This was part of the problem. I wanted to be likeable. This isn't necessarily a terrible trait, but we often sacrifice our own integrity for it. Being 'nice' to people while we're secretly harbouring resentment for them is a recipe for disaster.

The other option I initially considered was hardly any better. By it being just her fault, I could deny my own responsibility and give it all to her. I wouldn't have to get outside my comfort zone. I wouldn't have to push through any blocks, and I certainly wouldn't have to change my approach.

So, what does the third option look like? We respect each other and the mutual exchange by creating healthy boundaries – as difficult as it may be.

A boundary is like an energetic protection. It's a limit we set through our behaviour and choices that communicates to the world how we wish to be treated by others. When we have healthy boundaries in place, we know how to respond when people cross them. We also begin to respect and honour the boundaries others set. With healthy boundaries, we can step into other people's shoes, see the world from their view, and then easily switch back into our own shoes. This is enormously helpful, especially when dealing with conflict.

Boundaries are also about who you spend your time with and how much of your time and energy you give. For example, the fact that you're in the habit of regularly meeting up with your school friend doesn't mean that this has to go on forever, especially if your interests and lives have grown apart. Don't be afraid of loosening or even cutting cords if you might have outgrown certain relationships. Be super clear with yourself about who is in your inner circle of friends.

Our boundaries aren't always in response to someone else. Sometimes we need to create some boundaries for our own behaviour – for example, when we're trying to get more intentional about how we spend our time. Working on our boundaries is not only about protecting ourselves, shielding ourselves away and keeping others at a certain distance. Sometimes what we really need is to expand the borders we've created, allowing special people to come closer to us, physically and emotionally. However, that's only possible if we are able to change the dynamic as soon as the interaction becomes uncomfortably close.

Communicating clear boundaries is a way of showing up for yourself and protecting what you need to feel safe so that you can open up. If you know how to respect, communicate and live by your own boundaries, you will be far more confident in allowing and co-creating emotional and physical intimacy. Only a well-respected NO can invite and welcome a loving YES. Remember that you set the example of how you want to be treated. Don't expect others to respect your boundaries if you don't stick to or protect them yourself. This principle applies to professional relationships as well as friendships, and it becomes even more relevant in romantic partnerships. That's why I chose to see the challenge my colleague was presenting as an opportunity; if I could figure out how to feel comfortable with politely communicating my boundaries with her, I'd be much better equipped with this new skill when Mr Right came along. Over a cup of coffee, I expressed in a calm way that I felt let down. I apologised for not having supported her as I could have. Then I confirmed my positive intentions to make our relationship work and asked her what she needed to be more collaborative. What followed was an honest and insightful conversation that helped us to remove unfounded assumptions about each other's expectations. As a result, we were more considerate of each other's needs to perform well at work and our relationship became lighter and easier.

I think about the space within my boundaries as my personal 'joy zone'. When I am in this safe and protected space, I send my ego on holiday so that inspiration, intuition, spontaneity, authenticity, sensuality, creativity and other wonderful traits can express themselves freely. In that state, I feel guided, fully present in the moment and I can fairly easily access the magical state of flow.

Without boundaries, there is no safe and sound middle ground. All that is left is black-or-white thinking which suggests that 'all is either mine or someone else's fault'. These extreme positions put us out of touch with what is really happening and our power to influence matters for the better diminishes. This is catastrophic in romance, wherein we are tempted to see ourselves as the victim or the offender. If we view the world through the lens of a victim, we believe that relationships only work when we prioritise our partner's needs over our own. We resist declaring and defending our boundaries until it's too late, and then we overreact out of fear that our needs will never get met.

To completely grasp this concept about boundaries, I invite you to bring it into the analogy of Queendom. See yourself standing at the window of your castle and looking across a vastly rich, impressive landscape, with all its hills, forests and deserts. Imagine you are ruling over this beautiful country. How would you establish peaceful relations with other countries? Which atmosphere and culture would you create so that all citizens, communities, businesses, etc. would thrive?

You probably wouldn't allow a foreign army to invade your country on your watch. As a wise ruler, you would be sensitive enough to feel when something is off, when diplomatic relations with other countries are damaged and need mending, long before any army is sent. You would protect your country through building strong, trustworthy relationships with other kings or queens who share similar values and try to be on clear terms with those who have opposing views. You would react to early warning signs and if things turn ugly, you would protect your borders. But just as you wouldn't let yourself get invaded, you also wouldn't attack — nor would you withdraw from diplomacy completely. You would warmly welcome travellers into your country and treat them in a respectful, polite way.

Maintaining peace with other people's Kingdoms and Queendoms is a daily practice. You don't need to give yourself up entirely, hiding who you are; neither do you have to dominate and control everything for a relationship to work.

Live from the heart of yourself.
Seek to be whole, not perfect.
OPRAH WINFREY

So, buckle up and take a breath! Part IV is arguably where the most growing pains will occur. Stick to it, and don't forget that you're more than ready for the next phase to begin!

Pledge allegiance to your 'HELL YESes'

Make NO your best friend

If you want to create a life that makes your heart sing, it is essential to be crystal clear with yourself and others about what you say YES and NO to in your life. Most of us are quick to say YES and terrified of expressing a NO. Don't just throw your YESes out there as if you had 300 years to live. It's a fact that our time is limited. A quick and easy way to elevate your life is to fully focus your time and attention on the HELL YESes and treat every MAYBE or WHY NOT or OKAY, FINE as a clear NO. If you are invited to an event that doesn't excite you, don't go. Most things that seem like obligations are, in fact, simply options and it's fantastic to have an abundance of options available to you! At the same time, properly select what and who receives your YES. That's because every YES is a NO to another option at the same time. Life is about trade-offs. Learn to choose wisely.

Saying NO to people and things is a necessary step in creating a life that truly excites you. Think about it this way: every NO creates space for a HELL YES. This can be easy when you're making light decisions, like whether to watch a movie or buy a new bag. However, it's the uncomfortable NOs that really count, as this is where you're likely claiming back your sovereignty and energy. In other words, you're defending your boundaries!

Your daily life offers you plenty of opportunities to learn when and how to say NO and to stick to it. This skill serves you well when it comes to the ultimate test, which will be saying NO to a man who doesn't feel quite right to you. Life offers us lessons in YES and HELL YES when we make choices with our heart. Fascinatingly, the more we make choices and take actions based on our hearts' (or heart's) desires, the more life presents us with HELL YES options to choose from. We can build this skill up to use with Mr Right when the time comes, and it will only help our love grow deeper. In the meantime, we'll get to live as Queens of our Queendom, letting in what serves and gently but firmly keeping the rest outside of our realm.

It takes a strong person to remain single in a world that is accustomed to settling with anything just to say they have something.

ANONYMOUS

EXERCISE 22

An effective way to practise saying NO is a simple visualisation. Think of a situation you're in right now where you really need to say NO. If nothing comes to mind, find something in your memory. Consider a time when you said YES, then immediately regretted it. Now follow this exercise:

Step 1: Visualise the situation and hear someone asking you a question to which you want to answer, NO!

Step 2: Say NO in your mind or say it out loud. It can be short and stand-alone or it can be expressed in the following ways:

'Unfortunately, that doesn't work for me.'

'I'm afraid I'm not able to do that.'

'Sorry, but I don't want to.'

'No, thank you.'

'What other options are there?'

'We need to find another way.'

It may feel rude at first, but resist the urge to justify your decision. You can give a reason, as long as it's actually true and it feels empowering to do so, but know that you are not obliged to always explain yourself to everyone. Repeat this visualisation until saying NO feels easy. The next time you find yourself wanting to say NO, give it a go for real!

DIAMOND

It's time for a real challenge. Over the next three days, say three NOs each day that you find difficult to express. This can be anything from cancelling a meeting you never felt like attending, to not accepting more late-night work, to not giving in to demands from your kids.

Stay in your own lane

Let other people handle it

An important aspect of building your Queendom is setting healthy boundaries that protect your deepest needs. Don't live a life in response to other people's comments, opinions and random advice. You are so much more than that. You are a precious gemstone. Only you know how it feels to live in your skin. Your life should be comfortable for you. Once you've found your lane, learn to drive and stay there. Reach out to and connect with others, but don't follow them. We all have our own lane.

Asking for advice certainly makes sense in a number of instances. Be intentional about it. Have a specific question to take to someone you respect and trust and who is an expert in the area you need advice. In the same way as you don't go to a tailor to repair your shoes, don't ask Auntie Betty, who is a teacher, how to grow your online business. In most cases, the answer lies within. For anything else, ask an expert. Ultimately, everything should be your decision because you will have to live with the consequences of your actions.

The lesson here is more than shielding yourself from undue outside input. It is also about respecting and honouring the boundaries of your peers, giving them the space and autonomy to rule their own realms. If you connect from a sovereign, independent place, your connection can be more authentic, more real and more truthful.

Remember the 1987 movie *Dirty Dancing*? Patrick Swayze's character famously says, 'This is my dance space. This is your dance space. I don't go into yours; you don't go into mine. You gotta hold the frame.' Clear? No spaghetti arms. Hold the frame. This is pretty much how we want to dance through life with others.

When you realise your self worth, you'll stop giving people discounts.
ANONYMOUS

EXERCISE 23

Today you're going to honestly explore where you might be crossing other people's boundaries or taking responsibility for things that are not yours. Some examples might include:

- ✦ Trying to fix other people's problems.
- ✦ Giving advice that you haven't been asked for.
- ✦ Picking up the slack for others.
- ✦ Always making suggestions or decisions on behalf of someone else.
- ✦ Overworking or constantly overpreparing for meetings.
- ✦ Forcing your opinions onto others.
- ✦ Obsessively attempting to control a specific outcome.
- ✦ Cleaning up someone else's mess.

Grab your pen and journal. Write down ten examples in your current life that fit the above descriptions. Once complete, go through your list and answer the following questions:

1. What would happen if I took a back seat and let them take the lead?
2. In order to create my dream life, where can I better put my energy instead?

Knowing when it's truly appropriate to get involved and when it's safe to step away will support your efforts. That way, you'll never stray too far from where your heart needs you to be. If this approach to dealing with others is new to you, I suggest you repeat this exercise three times over the next month. You want to make it a habit to spot and course-correct when you cross other people's boundaries.

DIAMOND

This exercise probably revealed to you with which people or in which situations you find it particularly hard not to get involved. You have learned that your support might not be requested or may even be counterproductive in some instances. Pick the person or situation that challenges you the most and focus on letting go of control for the next month. Whenever you are close to intervening, consciously move your attention away; do something fun and meaningful instead. Break your bad habits by replacing them with a more appealing alternative.

STEP 24:

Uncover energy vampires

Protect your vital life force

Are you harbouring energy vampires? These are the people who always leave you feeling depleted after you spend time with them. Sometimes this can be a temporary situation, for example if someone we know (and want to support) is going through a challenging time in their life. Being at their side during a difficult period means giving them hope, lifting them up and holding space for them without shouldering their burden. This is a highly valuable service you may provide for close friends. However, certain people always seem to take more than they give. These are the kinds of relationships that dull your sparkle.

> **If you're not someone who has a natural and effortless love for yourself, it's hard to let go of your desire to please other people, and that's really not an ingredient for a happy life.**
> ANNE HATHAWAY

EXERCISE 24
Grab your journal and a pen. Write a list of all the people with whom you regularly (and significantly) engage, privately or professionally. Look

over the list and assess how you usually feel after spending time with them. Write a score against their name based on the following scale:

- **-1:**   Drained, down, exhausted, played, criticised.
- **0:**   Content, supported, neutral, seen and heard.
- **+1:**   Energised, motivated, inspired, deeply understood, happy, joyful.

If you have lots of people who scored 0 and +1, that is great news! Consider how you can create even more space for them in your life. If you've got mainly -1 people in your life, don't despair. Awareness is the first step to change.

Consider what you would like to see happen, and what choices you are currently prepared to make. You may need to reduce the time you spend with -1 people, begin to phase them out of your life, or even make a drastic cut. Just because you understand someone's behaviour, doesn't mean that you have to tolerate it. Your love for the people around you can be unconditional, but your trust and respect for others should be tied to their behaviour and actions. Accept that there will be times when you are alone in the elevator going up to the next level of your life. That's okay. Have the strength to go through that phase and see it as a great opportunity to get to know yourself even more. It's better to be alone in happiness than together in misery. Once you've cleared your inner circle from energy vampires, it's time to make new friends. You will have fun with the next exercise.

DIAMOND

Pick your favourite +1 people and arrange to meet each one of them over the next two months. Invite them for lunch or cook dinner and express what you appreciate about them. Even the best and strongest relationships benefit from regular nourishment and mindful attention.

Uncover energy vampires

Build your tribe

Extend your bubble

This programme puts you through a massive personal transformation. Don't be surprised if you realise that your current social circles need to expand. As you begin to change, it's normal for people who were once your closest peers to feel a little distant. Don't panic. As you free up time and energy previously spent with people who no longer align with you, new space opens for more like-minded relationships that help you grow and evolve further.

Empowered women empower women.

ANONYMOUS

EXERCISE 25

Grab your journal and a pen. What new horizons would you love to explore that your current friendships or communities aren't really up for?

This might include new skills you want to learn, places you want to visit, a spiritual practice you want to try, a new lifestyle, career or hobby. It might also be values or experiences you wish to attract within your close relationships.

Write down three new activities that come to mind. Now research the communities that will support you to explore it. This might mean attending evening classes, visiting wellness or health studios, joining social groups or taking up volunteering opportunities. Be creative and seek the spaces where like-minded people possibly meet.

Rank your search results according to which ones draw you in the most. Then visit the top two places on your list. If you like them, keep visiting and make an effort to mingle and establish new friend-ships. If you don't like a community, pick the next one down on the list. Do this until you are satisfied with your new hobbies and friendships.

DIAMOND

Repeat this exercise as long as it takes you to find three like-minded, inspiring, wonderful, fun, lovely new friends.

Take up space

Let yourself be seen

We all have areas in our work or private life where we shy away from putting our skills, opinions or abilities out there in the world.

This can show up in many ways: keeping your true feelings to yourself, downplaying your talents, letting someone else go first or not speaking up when you have something to say.

Playing small can be especially tempting when faced with people who always like to be the first in line. However, if you find yourself often holding the door for others, you can easily become the doormat. The solution is not to go to the other end of the scale, though. A constant display of domineering behaviour might get you what you want in the short term, but it doesn't help you with building long-term trusted relationships that are essential for a fulfilling professional and private life. You want to engage with life as it is, in a well-balanced, fair and non-judgemental way.

**We need to reshape our own perception
of how we view ourselves.
We have to step up as women and take the lead.**

BEYONCÉ

EXERCISE 26

Where in your life could you benefit from being more proactive?

This could be sharing your ideas at work, widening your friendship circles, expressing yourself more authentically in your relationships. Think of any situation where your true desires don't match up with your actions.

Grab your journal and a pen. Write down three situations where you're currently hiding your needs, wants or thoughts. Next, write down two actions for each scenario that will help others hear your true voice. Then, start implementing them!

DIAMOND

Do something that challenges you to step outside your comfort zone. For example, you could hold a speech in front of a big audience, put yourself forward to lead a project at work that you might feel is a touch too big for you, or openly share your feelings with a family member about a situation that made you uncomfortable.

Love your support team

Make a list of your best resources

Nobody needs to do everything on their own. No matter how confident, capable or strong we are, everyone is allowed to receive support. While our safety nets often only appear when we're in crisis, it's better to identify what and who we can rely upon before we really need them.

These resources might be people, such as friends and loved ones. They can be physical things like money, a hot bath or your own space, or services such as massage, therapy or an exercise class. They might also be within yourself, such as your beliefs, mindset or spiritual practices.

Your means of support can be accessed both externally and internally. They come into play in any scenario where you require physical, emotional, mental and spiritual help, love and care. Knowing your resources will give you a sense of comfort that you are not alone. You will realise that there is far more abundance in your life than you might have thought.

If asking for help makes you feel guilty or weak, please realise that the goal is not to do it all by yourself. The goal is to realise your dreams and fulfil your potential through leveraging resources in co-operation and collaboration with others. There are no brownie points in heaven for dragging yourself through life chronically exhausted and depleted because you wanted to prove to the world that Ms Superwoman can single-handedly manage it all. The art is to build up appropriate support structures, gather the right people around you, and use suitable tools and practices so that you are equipped in the best possible way to thrive and enjoy life.

Be strong enough to stand alone,
smart enough to know when you need help,
and brave enough to ask for it.

ANONYMOUS

EXERCISE 27

Grab a pen and your journal. Write down three headings: People, Possessions, Practices. Beneath them, list the possible forms of help you know you can rely on. Include anyone and anything that may be a support to you when you're feeling vulnerable, overworked, stressed, overwhelmed, upset or out of balance. When you're in such a state of misalignment, you may feel isolated. Seeing your options written down is a beautiful reminder that care will always be there when you need it.

- ✦ *People* may include family and friends, coaches, support groups, communities, counsellors, etc.
- ✦ *Possessions* may be a personal space where you can unwind and recharge, your journal, a savings account, an updated home security system, etc.
- ✦ *Practices* could be yoga, meditation, going for a walk, cooking, singing, chanting, dancing, journalling, various forms of self-care, such as having a hot shower after a stressful day, visualising a protective shield around you, calling on the Universe or your personal faith, etc.

Realising how many sources of support surround you may help you to feel safe and relaxed as you leave the ease and predictability of your comfort zone. Take a few moments to be deeply grateful for everything and everyone on your list. Isn't it beautiful to know that you are not alone – that a support network has your back?

DIAMOND

Actively nurture your safety net and support group. Once you are aware of who or what is on your list, bring them closer to you. Invite them for lunch, spend more time with them, thank them for being in your life. If you regularly check, mend and strengthen your safety net when all is well, you won't have to sew one on the fly when there is a crisis.

Trust that you are being guided

Have faith in a greater power

Ever feel like you're going around in circles — striving, persuading, pushing — yet the results that you've been hoping for are nowhere to be seen?

No matter how much we plan, work or try our best, sometimes things just aren't meant to be. Or sometimes we're in such a frantic state that we overlook the obvious solution. In moments when it feels like you're hitting a brick wall, often the most productive thing to do is the radical opposite: doing nothing at all and listening to the inner voice that arises in the silence. This tends to provide a surprising source of magic.

> **I searched for God and found only myself.**
> **I searched for myself and found only God.**
> SUFI PROVERB

EXERCISE 28

Grab a journal and a pen. Write down any scenarios in your life where you are currently trying hard to create a specific outcome with little success. This might be a problem with a friend or family member, a project at work, a personal challenge to overcome — any area where what you want isn't coming easily. Look over everything that you've written down, and now consider the following questions:

- ✦ In which ways could I consciously step back and trust a greater force?
- ✦ What if I let go of the urge to control the outcome?
- ✦ What if I simply surrendered my desire to the Universe?
- ✦ Could there be an alternative solution or approach that I am currently not able to see?
- ✦ If so, what happens if I am open to it presenting itself to me at the right moment?

Your next steps could be anything such as not sending that text message, giving someone space to think, keeping an opinion to yourself, delegating tasks or simply not responding. For example, if you believe the only route to success is to work day and night, the radical opposite might be to take a break and wait for new inspiration and a fresh perspective. Don't just consider it, do it! Next time a similar situation arises, take a step back, release control and trust a greater force.

DIAMOND

Let's dive deep into this lesson. For the next three days, become highly aware of your thoughts and feelings. Notice every resistance to tasks, people or ideas that might cross your mind or heart. The moment you become aware of them, note them down, either in your journal or into your notes app on your phone. As you write, imagine that help and solutions are sent your way. Now, relax.

Bonus Exercises

Congratulations! You've completed all 28 main exercises from Parts I–IV. I'll leave you with the final two bonus exercises. These are all about taking what you've learned forward and into your life ...

STEP 29:

Protect
your realm

Activate the divine feminine and masculine energy

Protection and support are basic requirements that need to be in place so that you can feel safe enough to express yourself freely and create the life of your dreams. Although we typically associate the masculine with protection and support, you do not need a man in your life in order to be protected and supported. Remember the exercises in Step 22 on setting clear boundaries.

Each human being has both feminine and masculine energy inside of them, and thereof both the divine as well as the wounded elements of each. At any given moment, you can activate one of the four categories.

The divine masculine energy is deeply present, non-judgemental, focused, fearless, logical, action-oriented, confident, honest, humble, responsible, accountable, and offers protection, boundaries, structure, security and stability. In contrast, the wounded masculine energy is aggressive, abusive, controlling, overly competitive, power-hungry, overanalytical, unstable and avoidant.

The divine feminine energy is intuitive, creative, playful, grounded, trusting, receptive, reflective, vulnerable, authentic, empathetic, compassionate, magnetic and strong. It flows through life effortlessly, surrenders, sets boundaries and stands for regeneration and transformation. The opposite to this is the wounded feminine energy, which is insecure, helpless, needy, co-dependent, impulsive, manipulative and overemotional.

	Feminine	Masculine
Divine	intuitive, creative, playful, grounded, trusting, receptive, reflective, vulnerable, authentic, empathetic, compassionate, magnetic and strong. It flows through life effortlessly, surrenders, sets boundaries and stands for regeneration and transformation.	deeply present, non-judgemental, focused, fearless, logical, action-oriented, confident, honest, humble, responsible, accountable, and offers protection, boundaries, structure, security and stability
Wounded	Insecure, helpless, needy, co-dependent, impulsive, manipulative and overemotional	aggressive, abusive, controlling, overly competitive, power-hungry, overanalytical, unstable and avoidant

The majority of the exercises in this book aim to activate your divine feminine energy so that you can fully tap into your intuition, creativity and innate power to create the life of your dreams, with or without a partner by your side. A couple of exercises, such as the following, encourage you to tap into your divine masculine so that you give your creations the structure, strength and protection needed to see the light of day.

> **What is the most beautiful in virile men is something feminine; what is most beautiful in feminine women is something masculine.**
> SUSAN SONTAG

EXERCISE 29

It's time to integrate the divine elements of feminine and masculine energy into your life. Draw a matrix with four boxes in your journal. The top left box is the divine feminine, the top right one is the divine masculine, the bottom left the wounded feminine and the bottom right is the wounded masculine. For each box pick three adjectives from the matrix above or similar behaviour that you demonstrate regularly. Over the next three days, observe yourself very closely and reflect upon the box in which you are spending most of your time. Once you've reflected, look at how you can balance things out.

DIAMOND

Many women look for men for protection of some sort, whether it's conscious or not. In order to feel whole and empowered, it is important that you activate your masculine energy and become aware that you can protect yourself on your own. Your body, mind, spirit, home and inner circle of family and friends are sacred spaces that deserve to be protected. Set your timer for ten minutes and reflect upon what safety and protection means to you in your current life. Be careful with your thoughts. This is not a moment to think worst-case scenarios and go into a downward spiral. That might even be the first learning here. Watch your thoughts and protect yourself from negative thought patterns.

Grab a pen and journal and note down three things that you can do to feel more protected. This can be anything from checking your privacy settings on your social media accounts, to buying curtains so that your neighbours don't get free reality TV with you, to cleansing your energy at home through smudging.

This exercise can trigger a lot. If you feel that this is an area that could benefit from additional attention, I suggest you work with a therapist, counsellor or coach to dig deeper and look at unresolved experiences of protection, support and safety.

Every end is a new beginning

Write your own fairy tale

Who would we be without the power of imagination? Is it not our imagination that makes life magical, special and precious? You are the one who designs the lens through which you see the world. Believe and you will see. That's how you create your world, not the other way around.

For your imagination to become a powerful tool in your manifestation toolbox, it first needs to be stimulated. As with anything, training is required to achieve mastery. That's why I would like to invite you on a fantasy journey. This exercise integrates everything you have learned throughout the previous 29 steps.

EXERCISE 30

Make yourself comfortable on your couch, maybe with a blanket and a cup of tea. Put on some meditative music. Set the timer for twenty minutes. Close your eyes and imagine that there is a Kingdom, a Queendom, an empire inside yourself.

Imagine it in detail. What does the landscape of your land look like? Where are your boundaries? Who protects them? Who lives in your country? Who do you meet as you go for a walk? Do you see the image of your throne? Who are your advisers? Who are your friends? Do you have any foes? What works well in your country? Which problems need to be solved?

The exercise is first to familiarise yourself with your inner land. Do you see a lush jungle, ice-cold rivers or an abandoned desert? In a second step, become aware of your responsibility for it, accept and embrace it. Thirdly, tend to your land. Maybe you have to mow the lawns, reforest, cultivate the areas around the lakes, feed wildlife, plant flowers or do whatever you need to do to feel at home and proud of your country, your inner Queendom. This a form of self-care that starts at the very core of your being in the immaterial world of your imagination. The way you manage and master your inner world will be mirrored and reflected in the outer world. If you learn to rule with love and care yet assertiveness and fairness, you will soon repeat the fruits of this inner labour on the outside, in the material world. Visit your Queendom whenever you are relaxed and happy or sad and overwhelmed and sort things out there first before you take action in the physical dimension.

DIAMOND

If you are very imaginative, take this image of your inner world out into your daily life. For the next three days, play around with it during the day. If you need help with saying NO, imagine knights by your side who protect and strengthen you as you express your opinion. To work on your posture and get an extra boost of confidence, wear an invisible crown on your head. If you find yourself in a situation where you are unsure about the next best move, ask what the Queen of your inner Queendom would do. Fantasy enriches your life. This playful approach will add extra spice and perhaps even miracles to your life.

Conclusion

Sometimes I get asked how my life has changed since going through this programme myself. And the honest answer is that most change happens gradually, with a few sudden shifts along the way. As with all transformational processes, there is hardly ever a clear-cut before and after. However, I can honestly say that my life today is, and feels, completely different compared to the time before I proactively started to transform it.

The most significant shift happened in regards to the importance I place on having a romantic relationship. I had realised that my life was on pause while I waited for Mr Right – that's why I started building my Queendom in the first place – but the actions that followed were what profoundly transformed me. Today, I experience a life full of joy and bliss. I treat every day as a blessing and I am excited about what the following day might bring. It's no longer a theoretical concept; I feel alive, with or without a partner by my side. What I was so desperately looking for in a partner for so many years, I found within myself.

So how important is it for me to have a boyfriend? It's still very important and not at all, at the same time. Despite this significant liberation from any external source of happiness, I still appreciate a committed, caring relationship with a partner I truly and deeply love, trust and respect. But today, my reasons for wanting to be in a partnership are purer, less self-centred than they were in the past.

From all the offspring of the earth and heaven, love is the most precious.

SAPPHO, THE POETESS

In the past, I wanted to be saved from myself; I wanted to reap all the benefits without having to do the work. Today, there are three reasons why I want to be in a healthy and loving relationship. One, I want to share the joy, love, and bliss I so often feel inside of me with someone who is emotionally and physically close to me. Two, I want to experience sacred intimacy with someone I love and trust. Three, I want to express the caring, nurturing and supportive side of myself towards a partner I deeply care about and respect. Despite these reasons, I am not desperate to be in a partnership as I know that my happiness doesn't come from or depend on being with someone else; it primarily depends on being in a healthy, caring, supportive relationship with myself.

How can I be certain that I won't fall back into old habits? The answer is simple: I have healed past patterns; I am grounded in myself and have developed a sense of what is and isn't good for me. This knowledge empowers me to avoid being seduced into an unhealthy, unfulfilling, co-dependent relationship. Certain characteristics that I used to find attractive in men now either have no power over me or even turn me off. I notice red flags much earlier and I have developed courage to act upon them.

Once you meet someone who ignites positive, warm, loving feelings in you, give the relationship a real chance by going for it wholeheartedly. Commitment is a game changer and it starts with you. If it isn't right, stop it – but if it is, don't hesitate to go for it.

Until that happens, enjoy life as it is and work on yourself. It's the best investment you can make. At a Kundalini Yoga training workshop, I once asked what I can do to attract my soulmate. The teacher smiled at me and replied, 'Many years ago, I asked the same question to my yoga teacher and got the following answer:

"The purpose of life is not to find someone else.
The purpose of life is to find yourself."'

This was an important reminder that everything begins and ends with us. We are here to grow as human beings through learning to feel and listen to our heart and soul and to connect with an entity, force, energy beyond ourselves. We are here to enjoy and evolve. Whatever aspects of your life you choose to develop, make it count, give it your all, go for it wholeheartedly.

Maybe this authentic, true, life-affirming, magical, soul-touching love that for years I had been searching for, found, lost, found, lost and been searching for again, had always been around me, inside and beyond me; only a heartbeat away, encapsulated in the next breath; accessible as long as I allowed myself to drop in, surrender, feel without fear, without judgment, without expectation.

I have arrived again at the point where I know one thing for sure: that there is a space where we are being held, loved and cared for just the way we are. A place where all is well, where everything matters and nothing at all, where time is an artificial concept of limited relevance, where energy speaks louder than words. A space we have free 24/7 access to if we dare to look within.

**What is a queen without a king?
I don't know, but let's ask Cleopatra, Nefertiti,
Hatshepsut, Sammuramat, Victoria, Elizabeth,
Amina, Tzu-hsi, and the countless other
kingless queens who turned mere kingdoms
into the greatest of empires.**

NIKITA GILL

On this journey towards yourself, I wish for you to experience feeling complete and wonderful just the way you are. I wish for you to experience magical moments of oneness with the Universe, awareness of consciousness, self-realisation and possibly enlightenment as you connect with divinity.

I pray for you to encounter and experience a love that makes your heart sing and deeply touches your soul and the core of your being in the most loving and caring way. My vision for the world is one where we have the courage to first focus on our emotional healing and personal spiritual evolution and then, as whole and emotionally mature beings, we meet and engage with other souls and hearts. No falling for egos and divas. Wouldn't it be wonderful if the foundation for romantic relationships were nothing less than pure love, respect, care, trust and support? With this vision in mind, I wrote the poem below. As you finish this book, it's my prayer for you.

And ladies, let's be honest. Once we've found Mr Right, the real work is only about to start. I do wholeheartedly believe in 'Happily Ever After' – not as a given, but as a result of consciously growing together through life and again and again, committing yourself to love. But that's another story.

May you experience a love ...

That kisses your soul and takes it flying.

A love that simply says YES without having ever heard the question.
One which knows doubt only from books.
One which doesn't ask questions but gives answers.

A love that is simply there,
day and night, yesterday, today, tomorrow.

One which begins in eternity and returns there.
One which has patience because it knows no time
but can move mountains in an instant.

It warms without burning.
It holds without crushing.
It glitters and shines like a sea of stars, pearls and diamonds,
without blinding.

A love that cannot be explained, only experienced.
Which is home and harbour.
Which offers safety as well as freedom.

A love that recognises, touches and renews your innermost being.

One which understands deeper than words could ever explain.
One which gently tends to old wounds and heals them with its caress.
One which laughs, cries and forgives.

One which celebrates both the feminine and the masculine energy.
One which creates a new Universe out of two equal, complete parts.

A love which holds the power of the Big Bang and is yet
gentle as a summer breeze, elegant as snowfall in the mountains,
colourful as a rainbow, refreshing as morning dew.

A love which makes its own rules and rises above them,
because it lives where there is no right or wrong, no black or white.
A love which has its own dreams
and wants to feel itself again and again.

I wish you a love which is not consumed by itself,
one which grows beyond itself and gives hope to others.

A love which strengthens, warms, inspires
and encourages everyone around you.

A love which not only lives in the fine, ethereal far-away,
but dares to descend to real, raw, everyday life.

A love which becomes human and vulnerable
but stays indestructible.

One which remains sacred and pure,
although it stands firm with both feet on the ground.

One which creates paradise on earth.
Every day anew.

Acknowledgements

A sincere thank you to all my friends who supported me through heartbreaks, disappointing dating moments, and who were at my side in times of unhappiness. You know who you are.

I want to deeply thank every mentor, spiritual teacher, coach and therapist, such as the most wonderful Dr. Gundl Kutschera (Vienna) who helped me explore and expand my inner Queendom. Special thanks also goes to Relationship Therapist Lin Burian (Vienna) for guiding me through a big heartbreak, Intuitive Healer and Life Teacher Fiona Arrigo (London) for deeply inspiring me with the concept of the Evolving Woman, and Life Coach for Women Nadine Spitzley (Zurich) for encouraging me to embrace and embody femininity in all areas of my life.

I would like to thank every man who I had the pleasure of experiencing elements of the rainbow of love with. Every rainy day made me value sunshine even more. My broken heart found a way to mend itself. This is the reason why this book exists.

My sincere gratitude goes to everyone who contributed their skills to this book so that its message can reach women all around the world.

A heart-felt thank you to Marie-Thérèse Czapka for so beautifully illustrating each single exercise, for bringing magic to the pages and thereby transporting the reader into the land of their own imagination.

Special thanks to Lucy May Taylor for editorial support, not least through many wonderful conversations about the joys and challenges of independent, authentic women in today's world.

Finally, a BIG THANK YOU to everyone who supported me throughout this process with patience, inspiration and encouragement.

About the author

Heidi Hauer is a Holistic Health & Life Coach for women who desire to bring health, happiness and soul-deep fulfilment on the journey to professional success. With qualifications in nutrition, holistic health and coaching combined with twenty years' experience in local organisations and global corporations, Heidi guides her clients to unlock the clarity, vision and self-awareness required to prioritise their needs and desires across their life, career and relationships.

In 'The Heidi Hauer Podcast' she talks with female entrepreneurs, coaches and professional powerhouses about how to be well while successful and how to have a positive impact on the world. She discusses topics ranging from courage to consciousness, from mindfulness to mindset shifts, from intuitive eating to impactful leadership.